Inspecto

on

Location

Antony Richards

All correspondence for
Inspector Morse on Location
should be addressed to:

Irregular Special Press
170 Woodland Road
Sawston
Cambridgeshire
CB22 3DX

✾✾✾✾✾ 〇 ✾✾✾✾✾

Overall Copyright © 2011 Antony J. Richards.
All rights reserved.
Typesetting is in Times font.
First published 2008.
Second Edition (Expanded and Updated) 2011

ISBN: 1-901091-30-9 (10 digit)
ISBN: 978-1-901091-30-4 (13 digit)

✾✾✾✾✾ 〇 ✾✾✾✾✾

Cover Illustration: Morse and Lewis on location at Mentmore Towers
(see page 26) in Buckinghamshire. This was the scene of the final rave in
the episode entitled *Cherubim & Seraphim*.
From an original watercolour by Nikki Sims.

✾✾✾✾✾ 〇 ✾✾✾✾✾

CONTENTS

Contents

INTRODUCTION

The city of Oxford is inextricably linked with its most famous policeman, Chief Inspector Morse. However, it may surprise the reader to learn that although much of the location work was done in the city, with many of the places being instantly recognisable to viewers, even more shooting took place outside of Oxford, and it is this aspect of filming that this book addresses. For instance Morse's own home, which is supposedly in North Oxford, is actually to be found fifty miles away in Ealing, West London while Lewis presently lives relatively close by in Twickenham. It is often fun, and sometimes frustrating, for the *location detective* to try and spot just where a particular scene was shot. Indeed as an example in the episode entitled *The Ghost in the Machine* in which much of the action takes place at the fictional Hanbury Hall two different locations were used for the same place. Morse and Lewis are seen inside Wrotham Park, near Potters Bar in Hertfordshire, and then exit for a walk in the gardens, which are actually those at Nuneham Courtney in Oxfordshire. The trick is to make it all appear seamless on the television.

The viewer is indeed fortunate in that from the beginning there was a desire by the production team to film on location as much as possible. This was a brave move since location filming is far more costly than studio work. When on location upwards of sixty-five persons a day will be on the pay role along with the added costs of travel and accommodation. Often scenes will be filmed several times, and even revisited on different days if say the lighting or weather is not consistent with the desired effect. For example in one scene it may be brilliant sunshine, but come the next day when the follow-on scene is to be shot it may be pouring with rain, such is the English weather. Since the location schedules are all set months in advance the only option is to shoot the sequence as planned and then return, if possible, on another day when the conditions are hopefully better.

The author can remember personally being present at the shooting of a key scene in *The Remorseful Day* when Morse and Lewis are discussing the case at a country pub shortly before sunset, with the former ending the scene by reciting part of the poem indicated by the episode title. The set up started around lunchtime with the first take being done mid-afternoon. To me, as a casual observer, it seemed to be faultless, though Chris Burt as producer had different ideas. Over the next ninety minutes there were many more takes done and only one of those repeats was because of an actor fluffing their lines; there was a man in the far distance walking his dog, an unwanted bird flying past, vapour trails from aircraft, the level of beer in Morse's glass was found not to be consistent with the previous shot and even the wrong kind of sunlight glinting from the aforementioned beer glass caused concern. In fact by the time the shot was finally satisfactory the sun had moved from being overhead to almost on the horizon. The version that actually made it to film though was perfect with no dogs, no aeroplanes and with just the correct amount of lighting. It lasted under two minutes and I wonder how many viewers realise just how long, and what attention to detail went into such location filming. For *Inspector Morse* there was around two weeks of location filming for every episode, and these production values continue today with *Lewis*.

Something else that does not concern the reader is that in a book the author may take the characters to any number of places, whereas when filming permission has to be sought and fees paid. During the early series of *Inspector Morse* the city of Oxford, both town and gown, were only too pleased to see themselves on the small screen. However, as time progressed and the series became ever more popular so this attitude changed. In the first instance the city actively tried to discourage shooting in the centre since it attracted too many crowds of onlookers. As a consequence some episodes had no Oxford filming. Coupled with this some of the locations realised that maybe they were not maximising the opportunity of such filming and started charging large fees. Oddly enough it was mainly the academic community who were guilty here, whereas the Randolph Hotel, which of course is a commercial business, has always been most generous in this respect being happy just to receive the added publicity (despite there being a suspected murder in one of their bedrooms!). These attitudes changed again when the council realised that Inspector Morse was a great asset to the city, and indeed made amends when Colin Dexter was given the *Freedom of Oxford*.

The problem faced by the author in writing this guide was which locations to use, and which to leave out. In our other book, the original and bestselling, *The Oxford of Inspector Morse*, the various central Oxford locations were revealed in a logical order so that the reader could actually do an Inspector Morse walk of Oxford and visit over thirty sites in a couple of hours. Here the sites are dispersed over many counties and hence are listed in a gazetteer fashion. The places outlined have been chosen since they either play a pivotal role in an episode and so will be easily recognised, or because the location presents a point of interest in itself which should interest the general reader. Most are accessible to the public and will make an enjoyable day out for all the family.

For now though - happy location hunting!

Antony J. Richards

6

INSPECTOR MORSE ON LOCATION

Here arranged alphabetically by county are over seventy-five of the most interesting locations used in filming *Inspector Morse*, and more recently *Lewis* (all five series to date). Rather than just list the places the author has tried to give the reader added information about their history, since each deserves an appreciation, and a visit, in its own right. In addition other productions are cited and where this is for a feature film the date is also included, whereas for television series just the title is shown.

London of course is a densely populated metropolitan area, and so here the author has tried to list places that are grouped close together, even though they may not always be regarded as key filming locations. Likewise it will be noted that although Oxford locations do appear it is only those few places that are not within walking distance of the very centre that are mentioned. Those city centre locations are fully explored in the best selling companion guide to this book, *The Oxford of Inspector Morse* (see under **References and Credits**), which is widely available within the city or direct from the publisher (www.crime4u.com).

INSPECTOR MORSE IN BEDFORDSHIRE

LUTON - LUTON HOO

[Side terrace and gardens where Morse and Dawson talk]

This country house on the outskirts of Luton is a Grade I listed building. Luton Hoo is not mentioned in the Domesday book, but a family called de Hoo occupied a manor house on the site for four centuries, until the death of Lord Thomas Hoo in 1455. Successive houses on the site seem to have changed hands several times until in 1762 the then owner, Francis Hearne, sold the estate for £94,700 to John Stuart, the 3rd Earl of Bute. Following an unhappy period as Prime Minister from 1762 to 1763, Bute decided to concentrate his energies on his Bedfordshire estate at Luton Hoo.

Stuart employed the neoclassical architect Robert Adam to design and build a magnificent house. However, this plan was never fully executed and much of the work was a remodelling of the older house. Dr. Samuel Johnson who visited in 1781 is quoted as saying, "This is one of the places I do not regret coming to see ... in the house magnificence is not sacrificed to convenience, nor convenience to magnificence". While Adam was working on the mansion the landscape gardener Capability Brown was enlarging and redesigning the park, some 1,200 acres. Brown dammed the River Lea to form two lakes, one of which is 60 acres in size. In turn

Adam's completed mansion was transformed by the architect Robert Smirke in around 1830, following the occupation of Stuart's grandson, the 2nd Marquis of Bute, to its present form today, complete with a massive portico. Luton Hoo is neither Gothic nor strictly Greek revival style, but an unusual example of a classical style for domestic use.

In 1843 a devastating fire occurred and much of the house and its contents were destroyed. The burnt shell was sold in 1848 to John Leigh, a Liverpool solicitor and property speculator. He rebuilt the house in the style and manner of Smirke with his family living there until 1903, when the estate was sold to the diamond magnate, Sir Julius Wernher. However, this was not before nearly a thousand Roman coins from the time of Caracalla to Claudius Gothicus were found on the estate in 1863. Wernher had the interior remodelled by Charles Mewes and Arthur Davis, the architects of the Ritz Hotel in London. It was done in the *belle époque* style that resulted in a magnificent backdrop for Wernher's acclaimed art collection. The marble-walled dining room was designed to display Beauvais tapestries, while the newly installed curved marble staircase surrounded Bergonzoli's statue *The Love of Angels*. At the centre of the house the massive Blue Hall displayed further tapestries, King Louis XV furniture, and Sèvres porcelain. Wernher's great art collection, equal to that of his neighbours in nearby Buckinghamshire, the Rothschilds, was later further enhanced by the marriage of Julius Wernher's son Harold Augustus Wernher to Anastasia Romanov, a member of the former Russian Imperial family, generally known as Lady Zia. She brought to the collection an incomparable assembly of renaissance enamels and Russian artefacts, including works by the Russian Imperial court jeweller Peter Carl Fabergé. For many years the collection and house were open to the public. However, many of the Fabergé items were stolen in the 1990s.

Following Lady Zia's death in 1977, the estate passed to her grandson Nicholas Harold Phillips, whose untimely death in 1991 caused its sale. The priceless collection is now on permanent display at Ranger's House in London. On 1st October 2007 the house entered a new era when it opened as a one hundred and forty-four bedroom luxury hotel, spa and golf course. Luton Hoo has appeared in many films including *A Shot in the Dark* (1964), *Never Say Never Again* (1983), *Four Weddings and a Funeral* (1994), *Eyes Wide Shut* (1999), *Wilde* (1997), *The World is not Enough* (1999) and *Enigma* (2001). Its singular *Inspector Morse* appearance was in *Second Time Around* where it was the venue for the Oxford Arts Festival at which Morse and Chief Inspector Patrick Dawson (played by Kenneth Colley) discuss the case on the terrace and walk in the formal gardens.

INSPECTOR MORSE IN BERKSHIRE

BRAY - BRAY STUDIOS
ST. MICHAEL'S CHURCH
MONKEY ISLAND
THE CROWN INN
OCKWELLS MANOR

[Entrance to St. Michael's Church, Bray. Visitors should beware of falling bodies from the tower]

11

Bray is a picturesque Berkshire village beside the River Thames, just south-west of Maidenhead. Indeed it won the 2005 *Britain in Bloom* award in the category of best 'Small Village'. It is famous as the village mentioned in the song *The Vicar of Bray*.

[The rather jaded Bray Studios as seen from the River Thames]

Bray is also known for cricket, fine food and film making. The cricket club is the oldest in the county, having been first established in 1798. Currently two of Bray's restaurants have three Michelin stars: The Fat Duck, which was adjudged the best restaurant in the world by *Restaurant* magazine in 2005, and the Waterside Inn, which ranked nineteen in the same magazine. This is particularly significant as there are only three triple-starred Michelin restaurants in Great Britain. There are also many television and film studios in the Bray area. Indeed Bray Studios were used in *The Dead of Jericho* for the shots of Alan and Adele Richards's house.

In addition Bray is known for several very expensive houses on the river upstream of Bray Lock. Notable residents include Gerry Anderson (the producer of such television programmes as *Thunderbirds*), Rolf Harris (the artist, musician and entertainer), Michael Parkinson (the television presenter) and Michael Winner (the film producer/director and restaurant critic).

Turning to architecture the Jesus Hospital is a red-brick group of almshouses, founded in 1609 by William Goddard, whose full-size effigy stands over the entrance, to house thirty-four of the aged poor of Bray and six of the Worshipful Company of Fishmongers to which he belonged.

The Church of England parish church of St. Michael was built in 1293, supposedly to replace a Saxon church at Water Oakley. It has a number of sculptures that may have come from the earlier church. It is best known to brass rubbers for housing the superb memorial brass of 1378 to Sir John Foxley, the Constable of Southampton Castle, and his two wives. One of the local cottages has a tunnel that it is believed leads to the church and served as an escape route for clergymen.

The church was the main filming location for *Service of All the Dead*, including the climatic roof scenes where Morse struggles with Harry Josephs (played by Maurice O'Connell), and again in *Dead on Time* where Morse interviews Helen Marriat (played by Samantha Bond). The church has also featured in *Midsomer Murders*.

[Anybody for croquet?]

Close to Bray just along the river is Monkey Island. It is associated with the 3rd Duke of Marlborough, and still houses two amusing structures that he built and furnished with paintings of monkeys. The island features in *The Settling of the Sun* as the place where Morse and Jane Robson (played by Anna Calder-Marshall) have a game of croquet.

13

[The Crown Inn, a typical Morse public house]

In the High Street will be found the Crown Inn. This quaint public house is actually far larger on the inside than its street frontage suggests. It was here that Morse has a drink in *The Daughters of Cain* and again in *Death is Now My Neighbour.*

[Entrance to Ockwells Manor or is it Chaucer College?]

Finally in the vicinity will be found Ockwells Manor that has been described as the most magnificent medieval secular building in the county. It survives almost intact from its original erection for Sir John Norreys between about 1450 and 1466. The timber-framed house has finely carved woodwork, especially the gables and patterned brick infill, and was probably built by craftsmen from Eton College. The hall is over forty feet long and houses the building's most famous feature, its superb heraldic glass installed by the builder. This displays the great Lancastrian connections of which Sir John was so proud (despite the fact that he switched allegiance when King Henry VI fell from power during the War of the Roses).

The manor had originally been given to Sir John's ancestor, Richard le Norreys, Queen Eleanor's chief cook, in 1283. The family lived there until 1517 when Sir John's great grandson had to give it up as a punishment for murdering one John Enhold of Nettlebed. The place was subsequently owned by Sir Thomas Fettiplace and his family and in turn by the Days, but by the late 19th century the house had almost fallen into ruin. Indeed concerns about its fate led to the founding of the Society for the Preservation of Ancient Buildings by William Morris. It was saved by Sir Stephen Leach in 1889 who began a programme of restoration, that was later completed by Sir Edward Barry. Today the house is a private residence and not open to the public. Five days of filming took place in the hall which became Chaucer College in the Lewis episode *Your Sudden Death Question* in which Marcus Richards (played by Alan Davies) hosts a fraudulent quiz weekend at which contestants keep dying.

ENGLEFIELD - ENGLEFIELD HOUSE

[Englefield House, hardly a suitable place for landing helicopters!]

Englefield village, near Reading, is mostly within the bounds of the private walled estate of Englefield House. In 870, the village was the site of a battle between the Anglo-Saxons, under Aethelwulf, Ealdorman of Berkshire, and the Danes, which resulted in a resounding victory for the Saxons. The battle was the first of a series in the winter of 870-1. The village is probably named after that battle: Englefield meaning either 'English field' or 'warning beacon field'.

Englefield House was the home of the Englefield family, supposedly from the time of King Edgar. Sir Thomas Englefield was the Speaker of the House of Commons. In 1559, the house was confiscated from his grandson, Sir Francis Englefield, a servant of the catholic Queen Mary, for 'consorting with enemies' of the new protestant monarch, Elizabeth I. The family later lived at Whiteknights Park in Earley but continued to be buried in Englefield parish church until 1822.

Popular local tradition insists, although there is no evidence, that the Queen granted Englefield to her spymaster, Sir Francis Walsingham. After a succession of short-lived residents, the estate was eventually purchased by John Paulet, 5th Marquis of Winchester, famous for his Civil War defence of Basing House in Hampshire. He retired to Englefield at the Restoration and is buried in the parish church. From his Paulet descendants, the house passed, through marriage, to the Benyon family.

In the late 19th century, Richard Fellowes Benyon rebuilt the villagers' houses as a model estate village and provided them with such amenities as a swimming pool, soup kitchen and a new school. Many of the Benyons have been Members of Parliament, including the current owners, Sir William, and his son, Richard Benyon. In 1832 no less than Constable was commissioned to make a painting of the house, while Richard Armstrong exhibited a watercolour of the house at the Royal Academy in 1873.

In *Twillight of the Gods* Englefield was the home of philanthropist Andrew Baydon, portrayed so expertly by Robert Hardy. There were both interior and exterior shots, and most memorable for the family was the landing and taking off of the helicopter which took with it most of the newly planted scrubs in the nearby flowerbeds! The house can also be seen in *X-Men: First Class* (2011), *The King's Speech* (2010), *Match Point* (2005), *Agatha Christie: Poirot* in the episode *Taken at the Flood* (2006), *East Virtue* (2008), *Marple: A Pocket Full of Rye* (2008) and the *Haunting of Helen Walker* (1995). The house and gardens are open to the public at certain times of the year and well worth a visit.

ETON - HIGH STREET
ETON COLLEGE CHAPEL

[Eton cloisters around which Morse and Hilary Stevens walked]

Eton can be found on the opposite bank of the River Thames to Windsor. It was originally in Buckinghamshire but due to boundary changes in 1974 is now in Berkshire. The High Street which runs from Windsor Bridge right up to Eton College is fortunate in that it has not been plagued by chain shops, although many of those present survive on the tourist trade. One of the premises was used was a bookshop in *The Day of the Devil*. The High Street has also doubled as the fictional Causton in *Midsomer Murders*.

Eton College, founded by Henry VI in 1440, is of course one of the most famous public schools in the country. The chapel, which is in the late Gothic or Perpendicular style, was never completed due to the War of the Roses, since it should have been a little over double its current length.

In fact the fan vaulting was only installed in the 1950s after the wooden roof became infested with death watch beetle. It was completed in three years and is made of concrete, faced with stone, supported from steel

17

trusses, with genuine hand-carved Clipsham stone for the stone ribs supporting each bay.

King Henry VI attached great importance to the religious aspects of his new foundation and he ensured that the services, of which there were fourteen a day, would be conducted on a magnificent scale by providing the chapel with no less than forty-six personnel composed of priest fellows, chaplains, clerks and choristers. Today the chapel services still retain their key part in the life of the college: boys attend chapel once on Sundays in addition to compulsory services three or four days a week.

The wall paintings, which date from 1479-87 and are in the Flemish style, are considered to be the most remarkable work of art in the college. However, in 1560 as a result of an order from the new protestant church authorities which banned depiction of mythical miracles they were white-washed over and remained unseen until 1923 when they were cleaned and restored.

In *Absolute Conviction* Morse can be seen singing in the choir, which incidentally is being conducted by Barrington Pheloung (the composer of the *Inspector Morse* theme music). Later Morse can be found in the cloisters talking with Hilary Stevens (played by Diana Quirk).

INSPECTOR MORSE IN BUCKINGHAMSHIRE

CHENIES - ST. MICHAEL'S CHURCH
DODDS MILL

Located close to Chesham until the 13th century the village was known as Isenhampstead being divided into Isenhampstead Chenies and Isenhampstead Latimers after the two lords of the manor. From the time of King Edward I this was an area of rich hunting and kings were known to reside here. Indeed it was King Edward III's shield bearer, Thomas Cheyne, who gave his name to the village and his descendant Sir John Cheyne who built Chenies Manor in around 1460. The manor house can be seen in the *Midsomer Murders* episode *Orchis Fatalis*, the *Rosemary & Thyme* Christmas special *The Cup of Silence* and the BBC series *Little Dorrit*.

[The resting place of the Dukes of Bedford]

The adjacent church of St. Michael's although not of great architectural interest does contain a fabulous series of monuments to the Russell family, the Dukes of Bedford. The church may be seen in the *Lewis* episode *Your Sudden Death Question* with the manor house also being visible in the background. It has also featured in *Midsomer Murders* as Aspern Tallow church in the episode *Beyond the Grave*.

19

[Dodds Mill at Chenies]

The River Chess runs through the valley at Chenies and gave rise to several paper mills. One of these, Dodds Mill, which was in operation for seven centuries until 1933, became the house of Michael Steppings (played by Brian Cox) in the episode *Deadly Slumber*.

DENHAM - THE OLD BAKERY

The village name is Anglo Saxon in origin, and means 'homestead in a valley'. It was listed in the Domesday book of 1086 as Deneham. St. Mary's is the parish church and has a flint and stone Norman tower and Tudor monuments. The picturesque tree-lined High Street has no shops as one might expect, but does include several old red brick houses with giant wisterias. Because of its unspoilt charm the village has been used in countless film and television productions and has always attracted those associated with the industry. Among the notable personalities who have been residents in the village are Roger Moore (actor), Paul Daniels (magician), Shane Richie (actor), Jess Conrad (actor and singer), Robert Lindsay (actor), Raymond Baxter (television presenter) and Mike Oldfiled (musician), while just up the road could be found Harry Saltzman (producer) and Cilla Black (singer). However, the most famous by far, and the only house to have a blue plaque outside, is the former home of the acting giant, Sir John Mills.

[Sir John Mills's house]

[The Old Bakery as featured in *The Remorseful Day*]

21

As far as *Inspector Morse* is concerned Denham was used as a backdrop in *Deceived by Flight*, *Twilight of the Gods* and *The Remorseful Day* (which featured two houses at opposite ends of the village).

DORNEY - DORNEY COMMON DORNEY COURT

Dorney, two and a half miles west of Eton, and referred to as Dornei in the Domesday book, is Old English for 'island frequented by bumble bees'. This refers to the fact that it was once a patch of hard ground in the middle of a marshy bog. It was on Dorney Common that George Jackson, the lecherous voyeur and handyman (played by Patrick Troughton), collects his blackmail money in *The Dead of Jericho*. Dorney is also the setting for Nicolas Quinn's house (Boveney Court) in *The Silent World of Nicholas Quinn*.

[Dorney Court, a mixture of Tudor and Victorian design]

The manor house, Dorney Court, is listed among England's many fine country houses and is a splendid example of an early Tudor manor house, dating from around 1500. The Palmer family have lived at Dorney Court for more than 450 years with the house passing from father to son in direct succession ever since Sir Thomas Palmer first moved to the house in the 16th century. On first appearances the building appears to be entirely medieval, but in fact some of the exterior is a Victorian reconstruction. The remodelling of the house was undertaken at the end of the 19th century and the original bricks were restored to the front facade of the house. The interior layout is little changed from 1500. The house is open to the public at certain times of the year and is well worth a visit (as is the adjacent garden centre which has a good tea shop and where you may also park your car).

In *The Service of all the Dead* the interior of the house is clearly featured as the workplace of Ruth Rawlinson (played by Angela Morant). The interior also appears in *Lewis: Expiation* but this time as Edward Le Plassiter's (played by John Wood) room in Merton College. Most recently it appeared as St. Gerard's College in the *Lewis* episode *Wild Justice*. Dorney Court is a great favourite for film producers having been used in no less than four episodes of *Midsomer Murders* (*Strangler's Wood*, *Bantling Boy*, *Secrets and Spies* and *Not in My Back Yard*), *Agatha Christie: Poirot* in the episode *Sad Cypress* (2003), *Elizabeth: The Golden Age* (2007), *Sliding Doors* (1998), *Cranford*, *Sense & Sensibility*, *To Kill a King* (2003), *Tess of the D'Urbervilles* (1998), *Agatha Christie Marple: The Body in the Library* and again in *Agatha Christie Marple: The Sittaford Mystery*, *Above Suspicion 2: The Red Dahlia*, *The Lady and the Highwayman* (1989) and *A Man for All Seasons* (1988).

FAWLEY - ST. MARY THE VIRGIN CHURCH

[The unusual rectangular tower of church of St. Mary the Virgin]

Fawley sits on the border between Buckinghamshire and Oxfordshire, about seven miles west of Great Marlow and north of Henley-on-Thames.

The village name is Anglo-Saxon in origin, and means 'fallow-coloured woodland clearing'. It was recorded in the Domesday Book of 1086 as Falelie. Sir Bulstrode Whitelocke, a prominent Member of Parliament in Cromwell's day, was from Fawley. In 1642 he allowed soldiers fighting in the English Civil War to stay at the manor house in Fawley, but they were quite raucous in their behaviour and completely destroyed the contents of the house. In 1684 the house was completely remodelled, following a design by Sir Christopher Wren.

The parish church, which was rebuilt in 1748, is dedicated to St. Mary the Virgin. Its main feature is a 'Tree of Life' stained glass window designed by the artist John Piper, who lived nearby in Fawley Bottom, and Patrick Reyntiens. The church was the scene of the funeral for the builder, John Barron (played by Jesse Birdsall), in *The Remorseful Day*. It was at the funeral that the wealthy widower Frank Harrison (played by Paul Freeman) is spotted in deep conversation with Liz Holmes (played by Annette Ekblom), who used to be his cleaner. Suspicions arise that there is more to this relationship than meets the eye.

███ ███ ███ ·█· · ··· █

MARLOW - ST. JOHN THE BAPTIST CHURCH
THE QUEEN'S HEAD
FAWLEY COURT

Marlow, from the Anglo Saxon meaning 'land remaining after the draining of a pool', was originally recorded as Merelafan. Little Marlow is around one mile west of the main town and consists of a group of village cottages set around a large open space, surrounded by lime trees. Little Marlow was once the site of a Benedictine convent dedicated to the Virgin Mary. The convent belonged to Bisham Abbey. In 1547 it was seized by the Crown in the Dissolution of the Monasteries and was eventually demolished in 1740. Today the village is in a scenic location on the River Thames and well worth a visit.

At the heart of the village is a manor house and next to this is the church of St. John the Baptist that fronts the River Thames. The original construction is Norman dating from the final years of the 12th century. This was the setting for the wedding of local village resident and former Spice Girl

Melanie Brown to Jimmy Gulzar in 1998. It is also a setting in the *Lewis* episode *Dark Matter*.

[The perfect Wedding venue for a Spice Girl]

[The Queen's Head – 'Marlow's little secret']

Also in the village is what is advertised as 'Marlow's little secret', more formally known as the Queen's Head public house, which prides itself on the gourmet food served in the restaurant. Although the place has since been extended to the rear this public house is still easily recognisable as that featured in *The Remorseful Day*. It is worthy of note that the pub is located at the end of a *cul-de-sac* and hence ideal for filming since the various vehicles needed for shooting need only block off a small section of road and so cause minimal disruption to the local inhabitants, while at the same time ensuring some degree of privacy while shooting. This public house has also been featured in Midsomer Murders (*Faithful unto Death*).

Finally close by along the Marlow Road is Fawley Court that also appeared in the *Lewis* episode *Dark Matter*. Filming took place over a period of five days with the building becoming a rehearsal room, shooting range, gun store and Porter's Lodge at Gresham College.

MENTMORE – MENTMORE TOWERS

[Mentmore Towers, an unusual venue for a rave]

Mentmore Towers is a large Neo-Renaissance English country house in the village of Mentmore. One of the house's former owners, Lord Rosebery, once said: "Mentmore Towers sounded like a second-rate boarding house". It is in fact a Grade 1 listed building. The house was built between 1852 and 1854 for Baron Mayer de Rothschild, who needed a house close to London. It was designed by Joseph Paxton who is most noted for being the architect of the Crystal Palace.

During the Second World War, the Gold State Coach was transferred to Mentmore Towers to protect it from German bombing. Trouble for the house began upon the death of the then owner, the 6th Earl of Rosebury, in 1973, when the Labour government of the time refused to accept the contents of the house *in lieu* of inheritance taxes, which would have turned the house into one of England's finest museums of European furniture, *objets d'art* and Victorian era architecture. The Government was offered the house and contents for £2,000,000 but declined, and after three years of fruitless discussion, the executors of the estate sold the contents by public auction for over £6,000,000. Among the paintings sold were works by Gainsborough, Reynolds, Boucher, Drouais, Moroni and other well known artists, and cabinet makers, including Jean Henri Riesener and Chippendale. Also represented were the finest German and Russian silver- and goldsmiths, and makers of Limoges enamel. The collection is said to have been one of the finest ever to be assembled in private hands, outside the collections of the Russian and British royal families.

The empty house, unaltered since the day it was built, was sold in 1977 for £220,000 to the Transcendental Meditation movement founded by Maharishi Mahesh Yogi. In 1982 the house become the home of the Maharishi University of Natural Law, while in 1992 it was transformed again, to be the United Kingdom headquarters of the Natural Law Party.

Finally in 1997 Mentmore Towers was sold to a company who plan to restore the house to its former glory and turn it into a luxury hotel and golf course. At the time of writing this process is still ongoing and the house and grounds remain closed to the public.

It is not surprising that such a magnificent setting has been used in making films. Most notable are appearances in *Eyes Wide Shut* (1999), *The Mummy Returns* (2001), *Slipstream* (1989) and *Batman Begins* (2005) where it was the home of Bruce Wayne (Batman). Perhaps its most bizarre appearance was in the *Inspector Morse* episode *Cherubim & Seraphim* where it was the location for the final rave scenes.

WEST WYCOMBE - WEST WYCOMBE PARK

West Wycombe Park is a country mansion, built between 1740 and 1800, near the village of West Wycombe in Buckinghamshire. It was conceived as a pleasure palace for the decadent 18th century libertine and dilettante Sir Francis Dashwood. The house is a long rectangle with four facades that are columned and pedimented, and encapsulates the entire progression of British 18th century architecture from early idiosyncratic Palladian to the Neoclassical. The finest architects of the day submitted plans to transform the older family house into a modern architectural extravaganza. Among them was Robert Adam, who submitted a plan for the west portico, but his idea was never adopted.

[The Temple of Music, a place to beware of the dog!]

The mansion is set within a landscaped park, containing many small temples and follies which act as satellites to the greater temple, the house. The park is unique in its consistent use of classical architecture from both

Greece and Italy. The two principal architects of the gardens were John Donowell and Nicholas Revett. They designed all of the ornamental buildings in the park. The landscape architect Thomas Cook began to execute the plans for the park, with a nine-acre man-made lake created from the nearby River Wye in the form of a swan. The lake originally had a Spanish galleon for the amusement of Dashwood's guests, complete with a resident captain on board.

The Temple of Apollo was originally a gateway and later used for cock fighting; it also screened the view of the domestic service wing from the main house, while the Temple of Music is on an island in the lake, inspired by the Temple of Vesta in Rome. Opposite the temple is the garden's main cascade that has statues of two water nymphs. The present cascade has been remade, as the original was demolished in the 1830s. An octagonal tower known as the Temple of the Winds is based in design on the Tower of the Winds in Athens.

[The ornate bridge over which Lewis and Hathaway run]

Classical architecture continues along the path around the lake, with the Temple of Flora, a hidden summerhouse, and the Temple of Daphne, both reminiscent of a small temple on the Acropolis. Another hidden temple, the Round Temple, has a curved loggia, while the Temple of Diana has a small niche containing a statue of the goddess. Another goddess is celebrated in the Temple of Venus, and below this is an Exedra, a grotto (known as Venus's Parlour) and a statue of Mercury. This once held a copy of the Venus de' Medici; it was demolished in the 1820s but has recently been reconstructed and now holds a replica of the Venus de Milo.

Today the house is open to the public during the summer, and owned by the National Trust, though it is also still home to Sir Edward Dashwood and his family.

It is the Temple of Music that features so prominently in *Lewis: Whom the Gods Would Destroy* for it is here that Catherine Linn (played by Sasha Behar) has her art studio, and also where later in the episode 'man's best friend' is set loose to kill the wheelchair bound Theodore Platt (played by Richard Dillane). Lewis and Hathaway are quickly on the scene and can be seen running across the bridge to the art studio, but are they too late?

This most picturesque of locations may also be spotted in *The Duchess* (2008), *What a Girl Wants* (2003), *The Importance of Being Earnest* (2002), the *Foyle's War* episode *Casualties of War, Cranford, An Ideal Husband* (1999), *Another Country* (1984), *Marple: A Pocket Full of Rye* (2008) and *Dead Man's Folly* (1986)

INSPECTOR MORSE IN HERTFORDSHIRE

ABBOTS LANGLEY - LANGLEBURY MANSION

[Presently not much hope or glory exists at Langlebury Mansion]

Langleybury was originally a country house at Abbots Langley (now better known for the nearby Leavesden film studios where the Harry Potter film series was produced) dating from around 1711 when Robert Raymond, then Solicitor General and later Attorney General and Lord Chief Justice of England and Wales bought the estate. In 1720 he demolished the original house and built the mansion that exists today. Evidence of his residence is still visible in the form of a griffin in a crown, his personal cipher, built into the stonework. In turn the house has been owned by the Filmer, Whittingstall and Loyd families but in 1947 the whole estate was sold to Hertfordshire County Council who converted the house into a school. A modern school building was erected adjacent to the main property in the 1960s so that the mansion could be used as teacher accommodation. The school closed in 1996 and apart from a short spell as offices for Social Services it has remained empty and in a state of ruin. It was therefore the perfect location for the television production of *Hope and Glory* starring Lenny Henry that was set in a school under threat of closure.

In the *Lewis* episode *The Dead of Winter* the house doubles as Crevecoeur Hall, the estate where Hathaway lived until the age of twelve and where he returns to investigate the death of Stephen Black who is found murdered on a tour bus visiting the house. The filming took three days with scenes involving the main hall, entrance lobby, great staircase, drawing room, bedroom and interior of the folly all being shot here.

ALDBURY – THE GREYHOUND INN
ST. JOHN THE BAPTIST CHURCH
ST. PETER & ST. PAUL CHURCH

[The church of John the Baptist in Aldbury]

Aldbury is the quintessential English village, nestled in a valley at the foot of a Chiltern ridge, close to the Ashridge estate (which is owned by the National Trust) on the borders of Bedfordshire and Buckinghamshire. In the centre is the village green, the pond and the Greyhound Inn, while close by stand the stocks and whipping-post, both in excellent preservation, a primary school and the church.

The church was restored in 1867, and is notable for the Verney Chapel, which is separated from the nave by a screen of stone, and contains a monument to Sir Robert Whittingham, who was slain at the battle of Tewkesbury. The church also contains memorials of the Hides and

Harcourts, families who left several charities to the poor of the parish. In the days of Edward the Confessor the manor of Aldeberie was held by one Alwin, the king's thane. This church was used in the *Lewis* episode *Counter Culture Blues*, but interestingly another church, that of St. Peter & St. Paul located just up the road at Little Gaddesden was also used for the same episode so that which appears on the screen is actually an amalgam of the two.

[The other local church, St. Peter & St. Paul, also used in *Lewis*]

The aforementioned Ashridge estate covers some 5,000 acres and includes a magnificent monument to the 3rd Duke of Bridgewater for his pioneering work on canals. Ashridge House was a one time home of Queen Elizabeth I and is now an exclusive management training college.

It will come as no surprise to learn that this picturesque location has been home to many a television and film production which has included *The Avengers* (most notable the episode entitled *Murdersville*), *Shillingbury Tales*, *The Dirty Dozen* (1967), *Bridget Jones: The Edge of Reason* (2004) and the very last Gainsborough Pictures film called *Jassy* (1947).

[Time for another drink Lewis]

It will equally come as no surprise to learn that on Morse's only visit to Aldbury in *Absolute Conviction* that he was not to visit the church, or the Ashridge estate, but only the Greyhound Inn. Interestingly he sits outside with Lewis to discuss the case with the production team importing tables and umbrellas bearing the name of an Oxford brewery to make it look like a local Oxford establishment (could this be an early example of product placement in television?).

BARNET - WROTHAM PARK

Wrotham Park, a 2,500 acre estate near Barnet, is a neo-Palladian English country house, designed by Isaac Ware in 1754 for Admiral John Byng, the fourth son of Admiral Sir George Byng, which still remains in the family.

[Hanbury Hall, also known as Wrotham Park]

Admiral Byng never had an opportunity to live in retirement at Wrotham Park for following his inadequately equipped expedition to relieve Minorca from the French during the Seven Years War, he faced a court martial and was subsequently executed in 1757 (for despite being cleared of cowardice and disaffection it was found that he had made an error of judgement and was therefore negligent for which the mandatory penalty was death under the Twelfth Article of War). This event was satirised by Voltaire in his novel *Candide*. In Portsmouth, Candide witnesses the execution of an officer by firing squad; and is told that "in this country, it is wise to kill an admiral from time to time to encourage the others".

In 1883 a fire broke out at the top of the house. The combined efforts of four London fire brigades could not prevent the fire from spreading, their pumps having insufficient power to throw water any higher than the portico and by evening the house was gutted. Fortunately, all contents of any importance were saved and the interior of the house was rebuilt using the same design as before, but incorporating the solidity of Victorian building techniques.

Indeed if Admiral Byng could stand today on the terrace of Wrotham Park he would notice surprisingly few changes, the house is finished and larger than he planned, the oaks are now mature and there is a lake at the bottom of the park.

The Admiral never married and left the house to the eldest son of his brother Robert (who had already died in Barbados where he was the Governor) and from him it descended to the present Robert Byng who lives in the house and has managed the estate since 1991. It is a private house though the public can visit on certain open days when guided tours are available.

Location scenes for Robert Altman's *Gosford Park* (2001) were shot at Wrotham Park, including exterior scenes and the staircase, dining room, library and living room. Wrotham Park can also be seen in several episodes of the television series *Jeeves and Wooster* whenever a country mansion (such as Brinkley Court and Chuffnell Hall) were required. The house also makes guest appearances in BBC productions such as *The Line of Beauty* and *Spooks*. Its only appearance in *Inspector Morse* is a memorable one as the home of Sir Julius and Lady Hanbury (played by Michael Godley and Patricia Hodge respectively) in *Ghost in the Machine*. It was this episode that sees Morse confronting the landed gentry. While Morse interviews Lady Hanbury poor old Lewis is left to question the servants. A vital clue is discovered when Morse notes that Hanbury Hall has something which Lewis's house does not – a flagpole on the roof! Interestingly although the interior and some exterior shots were filmed at Wrotham Park the body of Sir Julius (supposedly laid to rest in the Hanbury family mausoleum on the estate) is found at Nuneham Courtney (see under Oxfordshire) some fifty miles away.

-- --- ·-· · ... ·

HERTFORD - MCMULLEN'S BREWERY

Hertford is of course the county town of Hertfordshire and has a population of around twenty-five thousand people. The name is Anglo Saxon and means 'the ford frequented by harts or stags'.

The Rivers Rib, Beane and Mimram join the River Lea at Hertford to flow south toward the River Thames as the Lee Navigation after Hertford Castle Weir. Water is important for the main industry in Hertford centres around McMullen's Brewery that uses local water in its various products.

McMullen's, which is one of only a few independent brewers left in the country, was founded in 1827 in Railway Street by Peter McMullen, a Master Cooper by profession. As the business grew larger it moved first to Mill Bridge in 1832 and then to the current location in 1891. In those early days, Peter sold his beer to many pubs and individuals. It was not until Boxing Day 1836 that he bought his first pub, the Greyhound at Bengeo.

[McMullen's as it used to be, still worth a visit though]

The deal included three cottages on four acres of land at a consideration of £481. The 1891 brewery was built in the centre of Hertford along with the first well that was sunk to a depth of 140 feet. It took nine days to complete the job and cost £93-18s-8d. Since then two more wells have been sunk going down some 250 feet, maintaining a unique supply of natural water for the brewing operations.

A modern brew house was built in 1984, but in the mid 2000s the company had a narrow escape from closure as the controlling family was split between those who wanted to sell the valuable brewery site and those, led by David McMullen and supported by Fergus McMullen, who wanted to remain in brewing. Unlike several other family brewers, the result was victory for the continuation lobby as a clever compromise was reached. Several non-brewing property investments were sold to release cash and a plan launched to build a brand new, smaller brew house. The company would shed contract brewing and by concentrating on its own estate it could take advantage of tax breaks by becoming a smaller brewer. The new Whole Hop Brewery was opened in 2006 and being a more compact site the spare land, which included the old Victorian and 1984 breweries, was sold to Sainsbury's. Today the company operates around fifty pubs and almost as many again managed outlets, all of which are located in the northern Home Counties.

Morse would have approved of the product for in the mid 1990s the consistent quality of the cask ales was recognised when McMullen was presented with the first 'Brewer of the Year' award from the Parliamentary Beer Club. The following year McMullen's Country Best Bitter won the gold medal at the industry's international awards.

It is a little unfair then that in *The Sins of the Fathers* this is the filming location for Farmer's Brewery, the large international company know for its mass production of low quality beer. The location of Radford's Brewery, the small family run but struggling brewery with internal disagreements centring around the selling off of the brewery, was actually Brakspear's Brewery in Henley-on-Thames (see under Oxfordshire). It does seem that life is stranger than fiction for since making the production Brakspear's Brewery has ceased production in Henley-on-Thames and moved to the Wychwood Brewery in Witney. Unfortunately today much of the McMullen's brewery site is boarded up awaiting redevelopment.

LEMSFORD – BROCKET HALL
THE CROOKED CHIMNEY

Brocket Hall, which is a Grade I listed property, was built for Sir Matthew Lamb in around 1760 to designs by the architect James Paine. It stands on the site of two predecessors, the first of which was built in 1239. It is a tall red brick neoclassical house in a fine landscape setting with a Palladian bridge. The inhabitants of the house have never been ones to shy away from publicity and scandal.

Sir Matthew's son became the first Lord Melbourne and he was often visited at Brocket Hall by the Prince Regent (who later became King George IV), who had a liaison with Lady Melbourne. The next owner was William Lamb, 2nd Viscount Melbourne, who served as Prime Minister in 1834 and again from 1835 to 1841. Indeed his wife, the writer Lady Caroline Lamb was to have a very public affair with Lord Byron and was the person responsible for coining the phrase 'mad, bad and dangerous to know' on first meeting Byron. She is also memorable for serving herself up naked from a soup tureen as a surprise dish at her husband's birthday celebrations. On his death the house passed to his sister, who was to marry Lord Palmerston who also in turn became Prime Minister (1855-1865), and who died here while still in office supposedly on a billiard table while cavorting with a chambermaid.

[The magnificence of Brocket Hall, in many ways a miniature Blenheim Palace]

In 1923 the estate was purchased by Sir Charles Nall-Cain; he was created Baron Brocket in 1933. During World War II it became a maternity hospital. In the late 20th century Charles Nall-Cain, 3rd Baron Brocket, also a convicted fraudster and television personality, converted Brocket Hall into a hotel and conference centre complete with two golf courses. Although only accessible via a security gate it is possible to visit the grounds and walk up to the house since the hunting lodge in the grounds is actually an exclusive restaurant, the *Auberge du Lac*, to which the public may of book a table. You might even be able to stay in the hotel as John Thaw did while filming *Who Killed Harry Field?* as is evidenced by the signed photograph inscribed, 'To all at Brocket Hall. Best wishes, John Thaw'.

Various other filming has taken place at Brocket Hall including the BBC costume drama *Pride and Prejudice*, and films such as *Willow* (1988), *A Kiss Before Dying* (1991) and *Lady Caroline Lamb* (1973).

[It is easy to see how this pub got its name]

In *Who Killed Harry Field?* it is certainly an understatement by Lewis when he simply calls the place a 'nice house'. The security guard overhearing him comments, "You're in luck – he's flogging it. £8.2 million he wants for it". The 'he' in this case is Paul Eirl for it is his house that Morse and Lewis have come to visit with some lovely camerawork as the Jaguar, which seems so much at home here, is driven over the bridge and up to the main house where interior shots were also made. Literally just outside the gates to Brocket Hall is the Crooked Chimney public house which is where the motorcycle was found in the same episode.

St. Albans - St. Albans Abbey & Cathedral
Ye Olde Fighting Cocks

St. Albans was originally named Verlamion by the Ancient British Catuvellauni tribe. It was also the first major town on the old Roman road of Watling Street for travellers heading north from London and became the Roman city of Verulamium. After the Roman withdrawal, and prior to becoming known as St. Albans, the town was called Verlamchester or Wæclingacaester.

Running into St. Albans from the south is Holywell Hill its name taken from the story of St. Alban: legend has it that his severed head rolled down the hill from the execution site and into a well at the bottom (some versions have a well springing from the site at which the head stopped).

[The Abbey & Cathedral of St. Albans]

Actually St. Albans has moved since whereas Verulamium was built alongside a valley of the River Ver the mediaeval town grew up on the hill to the east of this around the Benedictine foundation of St. Albans Abbey. This is the spot where tradition has it that St. Alban, the first British Christian martyr, was beheaded sometime before AD 324. It was, at one time, the principal abbey in England and the first draft of *Magna Carta* was drawn up here, reflecting its political importance. The Abbey church, now St. Albans Cathedral became the parish church when it was bought by the local people in 1553, soon after the priory was dissolved in 1539. It was made a cathedral in 1877 when the City Charter was granted. There is evidence that the original site was somewhat higher up the hill than the present building and there has certainly been successive abbeys before the current building was started in 1077. St. Albans School, a public school which occupies a site to the west of the Abbey and which includes the 14th century Abbey Gateway, was founded in 948 and is the only school in the English-speaking world to have educated a Pope (Adrian IV).

The mixed character of St. Albans and proximity to London has made it a popular filming location. The Abbey and Fishpool Street areas were used for the pilot episode of the 1960s ecclesiastical television comedy *All Gas and Gaiters*. The area of Romeland, directly north of the Abbey Gateway and the walls of the Abbey and school grounds, can be seen masquerading as part of an Oxford college in some episodes of *Inspector Morse*. It is also where Morse sits and talks with Marion Brooke (played by Diane Fletcher) in *Masonic Mysteries*. Fishpool Street, running from Romeland to St Michael's village, stood in for Hastings in some episodes of *Foyle's War*. The Lady Chapel in the Abbey itself was used as a location in Sean Connery's 1995 film *First Knight*, whilst the nave of the Abbey was used during the coronation scene as a substitute for Westminster Abbey in *Johnny English* (2003) starring Rowan Atkinson. Finally the 19th century gatehouse of the former prison appeared in the title sequence of the television series *Porridge*, starring Ronnie Barker.

[The oldest Morse related public house in England!]

The road between the Abbey and the school, running down to the River Ver and Verulamium Park (on part of the site of Roman Verulamium), is called Abbey Mill Lane. On this road are the palaces of the Bishops of St. Albans and Hertford, and more importantly for the *Inspector Morse* enthusiast Ye Olde Fighting Cocks, where Morse and Lewis have a drink in *The Sins of the Fathers*, is situated at the very end. Note that once again that although this filming location is in a busy area that it is also in a *cul-de-sac* to ensure maximum privacy and minimal disruption to the public and film crew alike.

INSPECTOR MORSE IN LONDON

Greater London was used extensively in the filming of *Inspector Morse* and now *Lewis*. In fact to be accurate it is mainly the western boroughs that were used no doubt due to their proximity to Shepperton (and other) Studios where many of the interior shots were done. Most of the exterior film work was for what may be termed 'fill in' shots where the location was unimportant since it could be Oxford, London or anywhere else for that matter. However, presented here (listed alphabetically by borough and then by closest railway station) are over twenty locations each of which is of interest in its own right.

BOROUGH OF BARNET

MILL HILL – UNIVERSITY OBSERVATORY MILL HILL SCHOOL ST. JOSEPH'S COLLEGE

[Interior shots for the *Lewis* episode *Dark Matter* were all done here]

Situated approximately 9 miles north west of Charing Cross Mill Hill was formerly part of Middllesex having originally been Myllehill, meaning 'hill with a mill', in 1547. Two of its former famous residents are William

43

Wilberforce and Sir Stamford Raffles. Of the many buildings of note in the area perhaps the one of most interest to the *Inspector Morse* enthusiast is the University of London Observatory in Watford Way that was used for filming all the interior scenes in the *Lewis* episode *Dark Matter*, whereas the exterior shots were actually of the old Radcliffe Observatory in Oxford.

The University of London Observatory is a hands-on teaching observatory and is part of the astrophysics group at University College London and comprises five permanently mounted telescopes, two computer classrooms and a specialist astronomy library. There is a strong observational research programme in extrasolar planets and currently there is an initiative to expand the observing capabilities with the development of remote and robotic observing modes, which will culminate in a new large robotic telescope.

[The cricket pavilion used in filming *Deceived by Flight*]

Not far from here is The Ridgeway, an ancient track used and adapted during the past 2000 years by various settlers including the Romans, Saxons, Danes and Normans. On either side of the ridge the ground slopes steeply away to give spectacular views to Epping Forest and the Chilterns in the north and east, and to the North Downs and Harrow on the south and west. It is here that Mill Hill School Foundation occupies a 120 acre site, part of which formed the gardens of Ridgeway House, the house of botanist

Peter Collinson. Collinson was one of the most important importers of rare and exotic plants into English gardens. Many of the species that he introduced to Mill Hill in the 18th century continue to flourish today in the grounds of the school and do much to provide the unique and beautiful setting the school enjoys.

The school was set up in 1807 by a committee of non-conformist merchants and ministers who decided to place their school outside of London because of the 'dangers both physical and moral, awaiting youth while passing through the streets of a large, crowded and corrupt city'. Their foresight has provided generations of Millhillians with quite unique surroundings, peaceful, secure and rural and yet within minutes of links to Central London. Initially a boys only school, girls were welcomed into the Sixth Form in 1975, and since 1997 the school has been fully co-educational.

It is to the school playing fields that the *Inspector Morse* enthusiast must go for it was here that all the cricket scenes in *Deceived by Flight*, in which Lewis goes undercover as a worker at the University so he can infiltrate a cricket team and discover the murderer of Morse's old college roommate, were filmed. The school itself also doubled as a lecture theatre and shooting range at Gresham College in the *Lewis* episode *Dark Matter*.

[Holmwood Park – the mental hospital where Laura Hobson's roommate dies in the *Lewis* episode *Falling Darkness*]

As you approach Mill Hill heading north from London on the A1/A41, the sight of St. Joseph's College on Lawrence Street looms into view. The gold leafed statue of St. Joseph on the top (which was crowned by a special indult of Pope Pius IX in 1874) is a well known and much loved landmark. Sadly the college is currently an empty shell since the Mill Hill Missionaries moved out in June 2008. The college was first opened in 1871 as a seminary for priests training to go on missions to far flung places. Unfortunately the 1980s saw a steady decline in the number of candidates for the missionary life from the West, and this continued despite initiatives to accept any member of the general public who might seek such a vocation. The last student left in 2005, and consequently on the 20th December 2006 the doors of St. Joseph's College were closed for the last time to the Mill Hill Missionaries. The site is currently owned by the Matterhorn group who have sought to turn the location into a care home for the elderly. It was therefore the perfect location for the rather dark scenes filmed at Holmwood Park mental hospital for the *Lewis* episode *Falling Darkness* in which Laura Hobson herself is a suspect for murder.

BOROUGH OF BRENT

KENSAL GREEN- KENSAL GREEN CEMETERY

[The Doric porch leading to the chapel at Kensal Green Cemetery]

All Souls Cemetery was the first of the great commercial cemeteries to be opened in London. The General Cemetery Company was founded in 1830 and in the following year purchased 54 acres of land in Harrow Road for £9,400. A competition was run to design the chapel and entrance gates. It was won by H. E. Kendall with a Gothic design, but the chairman of the company insisted that it should be a Greek Revival construction and his will prevailed. Hence the Anglican Chapel has a Doric porch and flanking colonnades. Beneath the chapel are extensive catacombs served by a hydraulic lift. Among the good and the great buried here are Sir Marc Isambard Brunel and his more famous son Isambard Kingdom Brunel, Anthony Trollope, W. M. Thackeray, W. H. Smith, Wilkie Collins and Charles Blondin. The cemetery is of course open to the public and tours are given at certain times of the year by the Friends of Kensal Green Cemetery.

As far as Inspector Morse is concerned it was in the chapel that a service for Peter Matthews takes place in *Promised Land*. Matthews was a convicted criminal who died in prison and as such this funeral has attracted much attention including that of Morse and Chief Superintendent Strange who are seen with binoculars hiding among the gravestones.

BOROUGH OF CAMDEN
HOLBORN - BLACKWELL'S BOOKSHOP SENATE HOUSE

It is rare that a bookstore becomes a tourist attraction, but Blackwell's is not just any bookstore. For one thing, it lays claim to the largest single room devoted to book sales in Europe, the cavernous Norrington Room.

In truth, Blackwell's is not one Oxford bookstore, but nine, since there are separate shops for art, music, rare books, paperbacks, maps and travel, medicine, children's books, and a University bookstore. Benjamin Blackwell founded his store in 1879 in a tiny building at 50 Broad Street.

[Blackwell's Holborn store]

That first store measured only twelve feet square, and held just seven hundred used books. Blackwell's catered exclusively to the academic market, and gradually opened new stores in university towns throughout the United Kingdom. In *Lewis: Old School Ties* Nicky Turnbull (played by Owen Teale) is performing a book signing in Blackwell's, which is rudely interrupted when a bicycle is thrown through the main plate glass window. However, for this scene it was not Oxford that was used but Blackwell's (Business & Law) shop at Little Turnstile in Holborn which it will be noted is slightly set back from the main road in a quiet passage, thus making it an ideal filming location.

[The central tower of Senate House]

Senate House in Malet Street is the principal building of the University of London. It was designed by Charles Holden and built of Portland stone. It was opened in 1936 and was to have been extended further northwards to include Birkbeck College but the outbreak of World War II put paid to that idea. The massive central tower is two hundred and one feet high and was said to be taller than any building in Oxford or Cambridge so that London students could always look down upon their rivals at those other university towns! Today the building contains the administrative offices and the University Library of around a million volumes and four and a half thousand current periodicals.

There are also special collections of Elizabethan literature, economics and music. The building is closed to those who are not members of the University though tours are available by appointment and the building is often accessible during the London Open House weekends each year. Due to its art deco nature the building has been used extensively in filming everything from *Poirot*, to *Jeeves and Wooster*, to a James Bond music video. It was in this building that Susan Fallon (played by Joanna David) worked and to where Morse travels to tell his old flame that her husband has apparently committed suicide in *Dead on Time*.

FINCHLEY ROAD - CAMDEN ARTS CENTRE

[The Camden Arts Centre in Arkwright Road]

The Camden Arts Centre is a Grade II listed building close to Finchley Road Underground Station. The venue began as the Hampstead Arts Centre in 1965, part of the former 1897 Hampstead public library. It was taken over by the local council in 1967 and renamed the Camden Arts Centre. It ran courses for artists, and also showed artworks. Exhibitions in the larger galleries were the responsibility of the Arkwright Arts Trust. They were often ambitious exhibitions by well-known artists. These aspects of the centre moved away, along with most of the local artists who had frequented the centre, to become the Hampstead School of Art in 1992.

Following a £4.2 million refurbishment by Tony Fretton Architects, Camden Arts Centre re-opened to the public in 2004. The beautiful and sensitively designed building combines the original Victorian Gothic features with a contemporary urban design to enhance space and light. The new galleries attract artists of the highest calibre, able to display a broad range of work including installation, film and video, light sensitive drawings and sculpture. This was also the venue where Morse and Sir Alexander Reece (played by Barry Foster) talk about Dr. David Kerridge (played by Tenniel Evans) in *The Last Enemy*.

CITY OF LONDON

BANK - THE GUILDHALL

[The Guildhall Crypt, the colloquium room of St. Gerard's College]

50

As the home of the City of London, the Guildhall has been the centre of City government since the Middle Ages. The word guildhall is said to derive from the Anglo-Saxon 'gild' meaning payment, so it was probably a place where citizens would go to pay their taxes. The present Guildhall was begun in 1411 and, having survived both the Great Fire of London and the Blitz, it is the only secular stone structure dating from before 1666 still standing in the City. It is likely that at least one earlier guildhall existed on or near the current site since references to a London guildhall are made in a document dating back to 1128, and the current hall's west crypt is thought to be part of a late 13th century building.

There are even remains of a long-lost Roman amphitheatre discovered in 1987 underneath what is now Guildhall Yard indicating that the site of the Guildhall was significant as far back as Roman times. Indeed it was in the former underground toilet here that the body of Graham Daniel (played by Philip Middlemiss) is found, and also to where Morse tracks the discarded clothes of the Japanese student who has been so brutally killed in *The Settling of the Sun*.

The Great Hall is the third largest civic hall in England, where royalty and state visitors have been entertained down the centuries. It has been the setting for famous state trials, including that of Lady Jane Grey in 1553. The imposing medieval hall has stained glass windows and several monuments to national heroes including Admiral Lord Nelson, the Duke of Wellington and Sir Winston Churchill, while the Old Library building housed the Guildhall Library and the Guildhall Museum from 1873 until 1974, when the collections moved to the newly constructed west wing and the nearby Museum of London.

Beneath the Guildhall lies the largest medieval crypts in London and it was here that filming took place for the *Lewis* episode *Wild Justice*.

BARBICAN - IRONMONGERS' HALL

The Worshipful Company of Ironmongers has existed as a fellowship since the 13th century. It became a guild in the 14th century and was granted arms in 1455 and a royal charter in 1463. The early ironmongers were known as ferroners, supplying and sometimes making articles such as bars, rods, horseshoes, and cart wheel tyres. Although a Great Company it was also one of the smallest numbering around one hundred members even up to present times. The current hall is off Aldersgate Street and was purchased in 1922 and narrowly escaped destruction by fire in 1940. It is built in the Tudor style, recalling the Golden Age of craftsmanship, using hand-made bricks and iron fittings.

[The beautiful banqueting hall of Merton College?]

The panelled banqueting hall contains a minstrels' gallery and a fine Waterford glass chandelier. In the *Lewis* episode *Expiation* this building doubled for Merton College dining room (while Exeter College doubled as the exterior, and Dorney Court as another part of the interior).

CANNON STREET - SKINNERS' HALL

Like many other livery companies the Skinners' Company developed from a medieval trade guild and regulatory body. Specifically they were furriers who dressed and traded furs that were then, as now, regarded as luxury items. For example ermine and sable were reserved for royalty and the aristocracy while common folk made do with lambskin, rabbit and cat. The Skinners' Company was one of the first to be granted a royal charter in 1327, but soon these powerful guilds were in dispute amongst themselves, jostling for position and control over their regulatory empires that often overlapped. For instance the Leathersellers also sold skins, while the Tawyers treated and prepared the skins for making into furs that the Tailors sewed. The conflict between the Skinners and the Merchant Tailors came to ahead in 1484 when violence erupted during the mayor of London's river procession at which both companies wanted to be 'up front'. The mayor, Robert Billesdon, intervened and decreed that the two companies would take it in turns to lead the other in procession in alternate years, and hence the derivation of the phrase to be 'at sixes and sevens' as this was to be their respective places in future processions.

The original Skinners' Hall was destroyed in the Great Fire of London but twenty years later a handsome new hall was constructed on the same site at Dowgate Hill. Today it is a Grade 1 listed building comprising a courtyard, outer hall, court room, library, various committee rooms and offices, and the banqueting hall complete with minstrels' gallery. The banqueting hall doubled as that at Lady Matilda's College in the *Lewis* episode *Old, Unhappy, Far Off Things*.

The Skinners' Company does have one Oxford connection in that in 1858 the Company's barge was sold and spent its remaining years as a boathouse for Queen's College. Finally of note, in true Harry Potter style, the guest entrance to Skinners' Hall is officially designated $8^1/_2$ Dowgate Hill.

TEMPLE – WHITBY & CO.

[Left: The entrance to Whitby & Co., the 'Oxford' opticians]

Whitby & Co. in Fleet Street is far more than just an opticians that its sign suggests, since in addition it houses a variety of professional healthcare specialists all under the one roof. There is a private general practitioner, a chiropodist and podiatrist, a physiotherapist, an osteopath, a dentist, and a psychologist. Since 1983 Gillian Whitby, the senior optometrist, has built up a formidable record in understanding and looking after the optical needs of people working nearby.

The actual building is a carefully restored Edwardian former banking hall. In the *Lewis* episode *Expiation* this building became Mallory and Hayward, the Oxford opticians.

BOROUGH OF EALING

CASTLE BAR PARK - CASTLEBAR PARK THE DUKE OF KENT

[Morse's home is now derelict and awaiting redevelopment]

Ealing is not on any tourist map of London since it is mainly a residential area and one that is convenient for the central London commuter. Indeed much of the residential building boom in the area can be attributed as far back as the coming of the Great Western Railway and the station opening at Ealing Dean in 1871 and the later extension to Greenford via Castle Bar Park and Drayton Green railway stations.

The London United Tramways Company opened a line between Ealing and Southall in 1901 while the Metropolitan District Railway opened what was called a halt at Northfields in 1907. Hence much of the housing stock is Victorian and also reminiscent of those large properties found in North Oxford. Indeed recent *Lewis* episodes have used housing, as well as allotments, from this area to represent Oxford. Indeed this is where interior shots of the homes of Lewis and Laura Hobson have been filmed.

The best known property though is at 28 Castlebar Park (not to be confused with Castle Bar Park the district in which it belongs), a boarded up, derelict building and former squat awaiting redevelopment. It is a shrine to most Inspector Morse fans since this is the film location of Morse's flat and appeared in no less than six episodes (*The Silent World of Nicholas Quinn*, *Last Seen Wearing*, *The Last Enemy*, *Masonic Mysteries* (in which it was seemingly set alight), *The Wench is Dead* and *The Remorseful Day*). The house is quite unremarkable save that it has good size grounds and is in a quiet street making it ideal for filming.

Just around the corner from Castlebar Park is Scotch Common and The Duke of Kent public house. This Fullers' pub has recently been modernised (with help from the *Lewis* location fees!), and despite a few tacky touches, the overall effect is pleasant. The bar feels roomy rather than empty, and the huge garden replete with patio heaters is a delight in summer. It is certainly much larger on the inside than its frontage indicates. It was used by Morse in *Driven to Distraction* and has reappeared more recently in the *Lewis* episode *Old School Ties*.

BOROUGH OF HARROW

HARROW - HARROW SCHOOL

Harrow School, commonly known simply as Harrow, is an independent school for boys situated in the town of Harrow, and is considered along with its closest rival, Eton College, to be one of the finest educational establishments in the country. Harrow has educated boys since 1243 but was officially founded by John Lyon under a royal charter of Queen Elizabeth I in 1572, and even then the first school buildings, which are still standing, were only completed in 1615.

[The Old School at Harrow]

Harrow is a boarding school with approximately eight hundred boarders, all boys, each of whom belongs to one of the twelve boarding 'houses'. Such privilege naturally is not cheap and at the time of going to press the annual fee is around £30,000.

The school is world famous for its many traditions and rich history, which includes the use of boaters, morning suits, top hats and canes as uniform. It is equally famous for a very long line of famous alumni including eight former Prime Ministers (including Winston Churchill, Robert Peel, Jawaharlal Nehru and Henry John Temple, 3rd Viscount Palmerston), numerous foreign statesmen, former and current British Lords and Members of Parliament, two kings (King Hussein of Jordan and his cousin, King Faisal II, the last King of Iraq) and several other members of various royal families, nineteen Victoria Cross holders, and a great many notable figures in both the arts and the sciences. These have included Lord Byron, Sir Terence Rattigan and Richard Curtis. It is one of the original nine English public schools as defined by the Public Schools Act of 1868.

As might be expected the curriculum was rather limited at first with the primary subjects being Latin and archery. Also it may surprise readers that originally most boys if they came from the parish were taught for free, with fee paying pupils being those regarded as 'foreigners' i.e. those from outside Harrow. By 1701 there were two 'foreigners' for every local boy.

The school is made up of some 400 acres of playing fields, tennis courts, a golf course, woodland and gardens. The school also owns its own working farm complete with a herd of English Longhorn cattle and a flock of Shetland sheep, and until 2003 it was also a working dairy farm.

The beautiful and historic buildings of Harrow School have provided an atmospheric backdrop to films and television alike. This has included *The Saint* (1997), *Ladies in Lavender* (2004), *The Secret Garden* (1993), *The History Boys* (2006) and most notably, and appropriately, *Young Winston* (1972). Harry Potter was even educated here since the Fourth Form Room (in the Old School) appears in the very first film in the series as where Filius Flitwick's levitation lesson takes place. On television the school can be seen in series such as *The Professionals*, *He Knew He Was Right*, *Goodbye, Mr. Chips* and *Lorna Doone*. More recent filming has been done for *Foyle's War*, *StreetDance 3D* (2010) and ironically the docu-drama *When Boris Met Dave* about two Old Etonians, studying at Oxford. It was within the school that four days of filming took place for the *Lewis* episode *Your Sudden Death Question* in which Marcus Richards (played by Alan Davies) hosts a fraudulent quiz weekend at Chaucer College at which the contestants start to be murdered.

— — — — — · — · · · · ·

Borough of Hillindon

Harefield - Territorial Army Centre
The Coy Carp

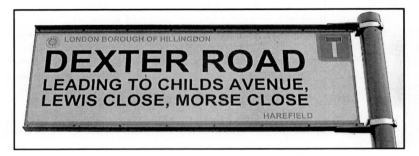

It is almost certainly unique to find a set of street names featuring people associated with a television series. However, in Harefield there are roads on a housing estate named after the author of *Inspector Morse* (Dexter Road), the Executive Producer (Childs Avenue) and the two central characters (Morse Close and Lewis Close respectively). The reason for this naming is quite simple since the housing estate occupies the ground of the former Territorial Army Centre that doubled as Oxford police station in several of the earlier episodes in the series.

[Famous 'Oxford' drinking venue not to be confused with Godstow]

Located in Coppermill Lane is the Coy Carp, a country public house and restaurant that claims to ooze rural charm and rustic character despite being part of a chain of similar establishments. It was originally known as The Fisheries and dates back to before the building of the Grand Union Canal. It is certainly a picturesque spot and overlooks Pynesfield Lakes as well as where the River Colne flows into the aforementioned Grand Union Canal. It seems that it is so similar to the Trout Inn at Godstow that in the *Lewis* episodes *Wide Justice* and *Old, Unhappy, Far Off Things* Lewis gets confused between the two, and even gets a kiss from Laura Hobson here on the bridge just visible at the right hand side of the picture.

UXBRIDGE - BRUNEL UNIVERSITY
UXBRIDGE MORTUARY
COWLEY LOCK

Uxbridge is currently the administrative headquarters of the borough of Hillingdon and has been a significant commercial centre from an early time. Negotiations between King Charles I and the Parliamentary Army took place here at a spot now marked by a public house called the Crown and Treaty. At the recently closed RAF station is the underground control centre for fighter command, Number 11 Group Operations, commonly known as the Battle of Britain Bunker.

[The place for examining dead bodies in *Lewis*]

In 1966 a royal charter established Brunel University and hence many of the campus buildings are in what has been termed the Brutalist style of that decade. It was this architecture that made it the perfect location for much of the filming of *A Clockwork Orange* (1971).

59

Various buildings have also appeared in *Spooks* and *Silent Witness* (where a college massacre occurs), and from series III onwards of *Lewis* whenever a visit to the mortuary is required the exterior of various Brunel University buildings are used, whereas the interior shots are all of Uxbridge Mortuary which stands opposite the main entrance. Brunel University was also the setting for the sleep laboratory in the *Lewis* pilot episode, *Reputation*.

[Cowley Lock not to be mistaken for Cowley in Oxford]

Part of the Grand Union Canal (opened in 1793) passes through Uxbridge at Cowley Lock while the River Fray passes through a culvert underneath the canal. To the north boats have to traverse no less than forty-five locks in order to reach Tring Summit whereas travelling south there are no locks between here and Camden some twenty-seven miles away. Hence in the early 19th century the Paddington Packet Boat took advantage of this fact and ran a daily 'express' service from here to the Paddington Basin pulled by four horses which had priority over all other craft. Both the lock, the Toll House Tea Rooms and a moored narrowboat (the *Whoopee*) were used when filming the *Lewis* episode *Dark Matter*.

Borough of Richmond

Twickenham - Cambridge Park

Twickenham became a municipal borough in 1926 and is best known as the home of English Rugby Football Union. From the 18th century until 1927 when the last powder mill closed it was also a centre for the industrial manufacture of gunpowder.

[Lewis's home]

After the 1818 Enclosure Award the area became a fashionable place to live due to its large town houses, and this is no doubt why the area has been used as a double for the town houses in North Oxford in the *Lewis* series.

In *Inspector Morse* the viewer never saw the exterior of Lewis's home, and then with the early episodes of *Lewis* he seemed to be living at the Eastgate Hotel in Oxford as this is where he emerges from in several episodes. However, from the start of *Lewis* series III he is firmly in residence at Cambridge Park, which is also the same street in which virtually every other suspect lives since no less than three other properties in this street have all been filmed.

CITY OF WESTMINSTER

LANCASTER GATE – ANGELUS RESTAURANT

In *The Last Enemy* Morse visits London and pops into the Archery Tavern (now the Angelus Restaurant) where he finds Deborah Burns (played by Beatie Edney) who wishes to confront Dr. David Kerridge (played by Tenniel Evans) who has a flat close by (in Cleveland Square), and whom she suspects has been instrumental in rejecting her appointment at the University. This is a rare occasion when Morse actually buys the drinks! Sadly the Archery Tavern closed in 2006 when its lease expired and the Church Commission, who managed the property for the Church of England, would not renew it. This pretty wooden fronted pub was in a *cul-de-sac*, just off the busy Bayswater Road, near Hyde Park. In spite of its location it always had a tranquil, country pub atmosphere, made more so by the frequent sound of horses' hooves on the cobbles outside, since the mews next to the former pub is still a working stables.

The public house was built in 1840, amid the continued rapid expansion of London. When built, the clientele would have been the servants and employees of the local households and tradesmen popping in for refreshment whilst working in the grand local houses. It was named after the popular sport and the Royal Toxophilite Society who practised at the butts nearby. In 2007, after an extensive refurbishment, the premises reopened as an up market French restaurant but still retains many of the original Victorian features.

[Angelus restaurant showing the adjacent mews]

PADDINGTON - PADDINGTON STATION

[The cavernous interior of Paddington Station at rush hour]

Almost within walking distance of here is Paddington Station which is the London terminus for trains from Oxford, and hence a place familiar to Morse. Despite this it was only used twice in filming. It is just adjacent to Paddington Station that Lucy Downes (played by Christine Kavanagh) is murdered in a telephone box in *The Wolvercote Tongue*. The second time it features is when Morse arrives by train in *The Last Enemy* clutching his *London A-Z.*

The original station was a wooden structure opened in 1838. Queen Victorian arrived here on her very first train journey from Slough in a time of twenty-three minutes, equating to 44 m.p.h. At the time Prince Albert thought that this speed was too high saying "Not so fast next time, Mr. Conductor". Some would say that the current management are still heeding his request! The new Paddington Station was designed by Isambard Kingdom Brunel and built between 1850 and 1854 and was originally for broad-gauge traffic. It was M. D. Wyatt who was responsible for the station ornamentation, and his elegant iron-work decoration embellishes the roof and capitals of the columns.

WARWICK AVENUE – ST. MARY MAGDALENE

[St. Mary Magdalene Church]

St. Mary Magdalene is the parish church of the Warwick and Brindley Estates close to Warwick Avenue Underground Station. When the parish was created in 1865 the area was overcrowded with poverty and disease being rife among the terraced houses. The church took six years to build from 1867, under the direction of the great Victorian architect George Edmund Street who was also responsible for the Royal Courts of Justice in the Strand. Although there is a broad south aisle, giving the impression of space, there is a strange false north aisle, which is in fact just a passageway. This was necessitated by the small plot size with which Street had to work. The ceiling was hand painted by Daniel Bell in 1873 and consists of an array of saints and biblical characters.

Coincidently one of the north aisle windows carries a particularly beautiful image of St. Frideswide, who carries a model of Christ Church College, Oxford, though this had no bearing on the choosing of this church as a location for the filming of *Lewis*. Indeed it was only the crypt, which was made necessary by the sloping nature of the site, that the film makers used. It consists of austere brick pillars and concrete vaults, with a massive retaining wall reminiscent of a railway tunnel. The crypt became the basement room of the Bodleian Library where Professor Gold summons Sefton Linn, Theodore Platt and Harry Bundrick (played by Anna Massey, Richard Lintern, Richard Dillane and Adrian Rawlins respectively) in the *Lewis* episode *Whom the Gods Would Destroy*. It again featured as a nightclub (albeit converted from a disused church) in another *Lewis* episode *Life Born of Fire*.

Other film and television credits include *The Blue Lamp* (1950) with Dirk Bogarde and Jack Warner, *Secret Ceremony* (1968) with Elizabeth Taylor, Mia Farrow and Robert Mitchum, *Poirot* with David Suchet, *The Constant Gardener* (2005) with Ralph Fiennes and Rachel Weisz and *The Oxford Murders* (2008) with Elijah Wood and John Hurt.

INSPECTOR MORSE IN NORTHAMPTONSHIRE

BRAUNSTON - BRAUNSTON MARINA

[Entrance to Braunston Marina with the village church behind]

The village of Braunston is situated on a hill above the main road and the canals, and formerly had a windmill, the building of which still stands but without any sails. Braunston's main claim to fame is its canal junction between the Oxford and the Grand Union (formerly Junction) Canals, that was once an important part of the national transport system. Many former boating families have links to Braunston, the churchyard in the village having many graves of boatmen and women.

The unique triangular junction between the two canals has two bridges made at Horseley Ironworks, and erected by Thomas Telford, carrying the towpath over the canal. This was not the original meeting point of the canals: the junction was moved in the course of improvements to the Oxford Canal in the 1830s, prior to which the junction was near where the marina is today, and where a third Horseley Ironworks bridge can be seen at the Marina's entrance. The marina was originally developed at the turn of the 19th century as the waterways depot at the northern end of the Grand Junction Canal. Several buildings date from this as well as the Georgian and Victorian periods. The canals are no longer used for carrying freight, but are now frequented mostly by pleasure boats.

As far as *Inspector Morse* is concerned some of the canal scenes, including the arrest of the boatmen on the *Barbara Bray*, in *The Wench is Dead* were filmed here. Other canal scenes were shot at the Black Country Living Museum, Dudley and at Honeystreet near Devizes (see under West Midlands and Wiltshire respectively).

INSPECTOR MORSE IN OXFORDSHIRE

Please note that this section covers the whole of Oxfordshire with the exception of Oxford itself which is dealt with in the companion book to this publication, *The Oxford of Inspector Morse* by Antony Richards and Philip Attwell (see under **References and Credits**).

BURFORD - SHEEP STREET

[Sheep Street in Burford where you should be particularly careful if working from a ladder!]

67

Burford, with its many antique shops on the main street, is located west of Oxford on the River Windrush and is a popular centre for tourists who visit the Cotswolds (indeed it is called the 'gateway to the Cotswolds'). The name derives from the Old English words 'burh' meaning fortified town or hill town, and 'ford' meaning a river crossing.

Of local interest is Burford Priory which stands on the site of a small Augustinian hospital. It is a fine example of Cotswold Jacobethan domestic architecture, formerly the home of William Lenthall, speaker of the House of Commons in the Long Parliament, who purchased the estate in 1637.

Today it houses The Priory of Our Lady, a community of Anglican Benedictine monks and nuns. Earlier in 752 Burford was the scene of a battle between Cuthred, king of the West Saxons, who prevailed over Æthelbald, king of the Mercians. In 1814 a large freestone sarcophagus was discovered near to where the battle was thought to have taken place. On examination it was found to contain the remains (in a near perfect state) of a human body, possibly Æthelhum. It is now preserved in Burford church, which in 1649 was used as a prison for the New Model Army Banbury mutineers who were held there during the Civil War. In all some three hundred and forty prisoners left carvings many of which can still be seen.

Between the 14th and 17th centuries, Burford was important for its wool that was sought for its quality and thickness. The Tolsey, once the centre of the wool trade, is located in the centre of Burford's High Street and is now home to a museum. Indeed in *The Remorseful Day* Sheep Street, which reflects the town's wool heritage, is the site where builder John Barron (played by Jesse Birdsall) is killed when he is knocked off his ladder while working on a house just opposite the Bay Tree Hotel.

DIDCOT - DIDCOT RAILWAY CENTRE

Didcot is approximately 8 miles south of the city of Oxford, and dates back to the Iron Age. The settlement was situated on the ridge in the town, and the remainder of the surrounding area was marshland. Interestingly according to a recent Office for National Statistics study, residents of the 1990s built Ladygrove estate in Didcot have the highest life expectancy in the land, as hence the absence of Inspector Morse from the Didcot area!

Apart from the nearby major scientific research sites and the power stations (which readers of *Country Life* magazine once voted the third worst eyesore in Britain) that are today a major source of employment for the town it was originally the Great Western Railway, which arrived in 1839, that put Didcot on the map, though it was not until 1844 that a station followed. The station enclosed the track completely in a similar style to Paddington but was to burn down later in the century.

[The main engine shed at the Didcot Railway Centre]

In fact the most obvious location for the original line to Bristol would have been the town of Abingdon a little further north, but the landowner, Lord Wantage, is reputed to have prevented the railway coming close to the town. This and the junction of the Oxford, Worcester and Wolverhampton Railway created the conditions for the future growth of Didcot. The junction became of strategic importance to military logistics, in particular during the campaign on the Western Front and the build up to D-Day. Although that railway line has closed and the large Army and Royal Air Force ordnance depots that were built to serve these needs have long since disappeared beneath the power station and the Milton Park trading estate, there is still an army camp (Vauxhall Barracks) on the edge of town.

As the car became the preferred mode of transport so the railway declined with the station becoming Didcot Parkway with large areas of the original sidings becoming a car park. However, the locomotive depot was saved and became part of the Didcot Railway Centre (run by the Great Western Society) in 1967. The Society has a comprehensive collection of Great Western Railway locomotives and rolling stock. There are two short lengths of running track, both with a station at each end.

The shorter of the two lengths, the 'branch line', has a wayside halt-type station named Didcot Halt at one end while at the other is the trans-shipment shed dating from broad gauge days, when it was used for transferring goods from broad to narrow gauge rolling stock and vice versa; it has been carefully reconstructed from its original site nearby.

The other length of track has a prefabricated concrete station platform (from Eynsham) at one end next to the entrance, and a newly built platform at the other. Long-term plans include the reconstruction of the Brunel station building from Upper Heyford on this platform. The site retains many original features including the engine shed, turntable pit and coal stage from the 1932 rebuilding.

The centre regularly holds events such as steam and diesel railcar days and in *The Wolvercote Tongue* it is Howard Brown (played by Bill Reimbold), a suspect in the death of Laura Poindexter (played by Christine Norden), who visits one such event. Lewis secretly follows him as he makes his excuses of not feeling well at the beginning of an Oxford tour at the Martyrs' Memorial. Lewis follows him to Didcot where Brown enjoys the steam trains. Lewis then radios Morse to join him. They then question Brown as to his strange actions. He explains that he was a civil engineer and that because his wife thinks of his interests as childish, he would sometimes feign illness to visit sites of interest. Morse and Lewis also question him as to what Eddie Poindexter stood to gain when his wife, Laura, died. Later on the platform at Didcot Parkway, Howard Brown sees the missing Eddie Poindexter (played by Robert Arden) with his long-lost daughter departing on a train and captures this scene on his camcorder.

GODSTOW - THE TROUT INN

Godstow is now mainly known for the ruined Godstow Abbey (also known as Godstow Nunnery). It was built on what was then an island between streams running into the River Thames. The site was given to Edith, widow of Sir William Launceline in 1133 by John of St. John and built in local limestone in honour of St. Mary and St. John the Baptist for nuns of the Benedictine Order; with a further gift of land from him, the site was later enlarged. The church was consecrated in 1139, and twice more enlarged in 1176 and 1188. The abbey became the final burial place of the famed beauty Rosamund Clifford, the long-term mistress of King Henry II. His liaison with Rosamund became public knowledge in 1174; it ended when she retired to the nunnery at Godstow in 1176, shortly before her death.

The abbey became a victim of the Dissolution of the Monasteries in 1539 and was converted into Godstow House by George Owen. It was occupied by his family until 1645, when the building was badly damaged in the Civil War. After this damage, the building fell into disrepair and was used by the locals as a source of stone for their buildings.

[The ever-popular Trout Inn at Godstow]

Godstow is also known for the Trout Inn situated in Godstow Road, Godstow, Lower Wolvercote opposite the ruined abbey. It was originally a fisherman's house built in the 16th century. By 1625 it was an inn and was rebuilt in 1737 incorporating separate stables that are still visible. During the Civil War, Parliamentarian troops from Banbury were sent to arrest 'a gentleman of quality', possibly a David Walter, who had fortified the building for the King. By May 1645 he had to evacuate, and it was put to the torch, but not completely destroyed, as the Roundheads were later to occupy it. Walter survived these troubled times, and was noted in the tax records for 1662. By 1720, most of the abbey grange across the river had been demolished and the stone used to extend the house. The present two-storey building of grey stone and pitched roof of Stonesfield slate contains flag stoned rooms, large oak beams, fireplaces and leaded windows. It is famous for its wandering peacocks, its river terrace and is mentioned in Matthew Arnold's poem *The Scholar Gipsy*.

The Trout Inn and Wolvercote are pivotal places in *The Jewel That Was Ours*, dramatised as *The Wolvercote Tongue*. The gold Saxon buckle was found at Wolvercote in 1931 and the later discovery of the matching tongue in an American collection bring about a perplexing chain of events. The dramatisation finds Morse and Lewis on the bridge by the pub, with Morse insisting on a connection between the theft of the tongue and the death of its owner, Laura Poindexter (played by Christine Norden). Eddie Poindexter (played by Robert Arden) later explains to Morse, at a riverside table, about his peculiar behaviour and the jewel's disappearance. The concluding scene has Morse and Lewis back at he Trout Inn, when, with a little 'Athurian' flourish, the Wolvercote Tongue is found by a diver; conversely in the novel, divers spent four days there looking for the jewel that Eddie had in fact hidden in the silk lining of Laura's coffin. It is also the location where Morse says that if anybody wanted to find him they may do so there "looking at fish through the bottom of a beer glass".

The pub has also featured in *The Service of All the Dead*, *The Sins of the Fathers*, *Who Killed Harry Field?* and *Second Time Around*.

HENLEY-ON-THAMES - BRAKSPEAR'S BREWERY

[The old Brakspear's Brewery, now a luxury hotel]

The first record of a medieval settlement at Henley-on-Thames dates to 1179 and King Henry I. By the beginning of the 16th century the town extended along the west bank of the River Thames from Friday Street in the south to the manor, now Phyllis Court, in the north and took in Hart Street and New Street. Henley suffered from both sides in the Civil War, though it prospered in the late 17th and 18th centuries due to the manufacture of glass and malt, and trade in corn and wool.

Henley-on-Thames has always attracted the wealthy. Dusty Springfield, the singer, lived and died here and even has a gravesite and marker in the grounds of St. Mary the Virgin Church. Author George Orwell spent some of his formative years in Henley-on-Thames while Humphrey Gainsborough, brother of the artist Thomas Gainsborough, was a pastor and inventor who lived here. George Harrison, the musician, lived in the town from the 1970s until his death in 2001.

[Colin Dexter poses in Morse's Jaguar outside the brew house entrance at Brakspear's Brewery just prior to the launch of a special beer entitled *Morse's Bitter Endeavour*]

Another name associated with Henley-on-Thames is Brakspear. It was in 1711 that W. H. Brakspear bought a brewery in Bell Street. The family are distantly related to Nicholas Breakspear, who became Pope Adrian IV in 1154 — the only Englishman to become Pope. In 1812 the brewery moved to New Street where it remained until 2002, when the brewing operations were sold and moved to the Wychwood Brewery in Witney, Oxfordshire. The site was subsequently sold and converted into part of the Hotel du Vin chain of boutique hotels.

Brakspear's beer is brewed using the traditional double drop fermentation method. This involves allowing fermentation to start in vessels on an upper floor, then the following morning 'dropping' the fermenting beer into a second vessel below. This leaves tired or dead yeast and unwanted solids ('trub') behind and encourages a healthier fermentation. It is claimed that all Brakspear beers possess a butterscotch flavour due to a natural compound – diacetyl produced through this method and their particular long-lived, multi-strain yeast, thought to have originally come from a defunct London brewery.

Brakspear's Brewery was used extensively in the filming of *The Sins of the Fathers* being renamed Radford Brewery for the story. Radford Brewery began in 1841, holds a secret or two, and is still in the hands of the Radford family. The opening scenes find Trevor Radford (played by Andy Bradford), the current managing director, working late in the brewery. He types a letter to his solicitor, curiously dated three years ago, burns the copy, and places the original in the safe. Then, as he walks down the stairs, he is attacked with a mallet and murdered by an unknown assailant.

Much of the questioning naturally takes place at the brewery as we also learn that the Radford family are in financial trouble and a larger rival brewery, Farmers (see under Hertfordshire), are offering to purchase the business. Trevor's brother, Steven (played by Paul Shelley), steps in to find the extent of the brewery's problems, whilst amongst the senior staff, Norman Weeks (played by Simon Slater) and Victor Preece (played by Alex Jennings) jockey for position.

Two more murders follow, including another Radford found dead at the brewery, before Morse can unravel a tangled web of blackmail, Victorian scandal, secret money dealings and disputed inheritance to discover the truth. At the end of the case when Lewis invites Morse for a pint he muses that he is "not absolutely sure". He does!

KIDLINGTON - THAMES VALLEY POLICE H.Q.

Kidlington lies in the centre of Oxfordshire on the River Cherwell, which rises in Northamptonshire and forms one of the tributaries of the River Thames. The name Kidlington was derived from the 'tun' (Anglo-Saxon for settlement or farm) of Cydela. The first written form of the name appears in the Domesday Book of 1086 as Chedelintone. By about 1130 it is found in the form Kedelinton. Today it is a contender for the largest village in England with a population of around fourteen thousand people.

Perhaps the oldest building in Kidlington is St. Mary's Church to be found, appropriately enough, in Church Street. At one time this was a busy working area with shops, but today it is a quiet residential road. The church dates from circa 1220, but was built on the foundations of an earlier church of Norman or Saxon times. It was constructed in the Early English style but altered extensively in the 15th century, when the upper stages of the tower and spire rising one hundred and seventy feet above it were added. Nearby are some almshouses built by Sir William Morton, in 1671, and endowed under the provisions of his will. The Morton coat of arms is visible at the north end of the house, and the names of some of the Morton children are on the window ledges.

[Aspects of the rather functional Thames Valley Police Headquarters South building in Kidlington]

Associated with Kidlington are Sir John Vanbrugh, the architect, who lived here during the building of Blenheim Palace, Thomas Beecham who formulated his medicine while working for a time as a gardener to Sir John Sydenham and finally Sir Richard Branson who still maintains a property here.

Although never used in filming Kidlington is the real life headquarters for the Thames Valley Police and is therefore also the base of operations for Morse and Lewis, being the site of Morse's office in the books. Morse was even held in the cells here (though filmed at Harefield – see under Borough of Hillingdon, London) when he was framed for murder by the arch-villain, Hugo de Vries (played by Ian McDiarmid) in *Masonic Mysteries*.

NUNEHAM COURTNEY - ALL SAINTS OLD CHURCH

[The Hanbury family mausoleum]

Nuneham Courtenay lies about five miles south-east of Oxford. In the 1760s Simon Harcourt, 1st Earl of Harcourt, demolished the old village in order to create a landscaped park around his new villa. He removed the village in its entirety, and recreated it along the main Oxford road.

76

The Harcourt Arboretum lies just outside the village and is part of the tree and plant collection of Oxford University's Oxford Botanic Garden. It occupies part of what were the grounds of Nuneham House. The arboretum includes 10 acres of woodland as well as 37 acres of wild flower meadow and is open to the public at certain times of the year.

The village is also home to the Bodleian Library's Nuneham Courtenay book repository, which houses one and a half million items selected from the University of Oxford's collections within what was the Victorian village church.

Nuneham House is a Palladian villa, built Simon Harcourt in 1756 with grounds landscaped by Capability Brown. During the Second World War it was requisitioned by the Ministry of Defence and became RAF Nuneham Park, a photographic reconnaissance interpretation unit. The RAF Station continued after the war in the same role until the mid 1950s, when the added buildings and roadways were demolished and the estate handed back to the Harcourt family who later sold much of the estate to the Oxford University Chest. The house though is presently administered by the Brahma Kumaris World Spiritual University that runs residential retreats, lectures and seminars here.

All Saints Old Church, to give it its formal title, was built by the first Lord Harcourt after he had demolished the original village church. It was designed as a domed Palladian temple overlooking the River Thames and is situated close to the house. It is possible to make a visit by prior arrangement. It was this church that in *Ghost in the Machine* was the Hanbury family mausoleum and where the body of Sir Julius Hanbury (played by Michael Godley) was found by Morse. Although some of the garden and mausoleum scenes were filmed here the actual location of Hanbury Hall is Wrotham Park (see under Hertfordshire).

OLD MARSTON - THE VICTORIA ARMS
THE MANOR HOUSE

Marston, or more correctly Old Marston, is situated to the north-east of Oxford on the River Cherwell, and is probably a corruption of 'marsh town'. The first mention of a church at Marston is in a charter of 1122 by which the chapel of Marston was granted to the Augustinian canons of St. Frideswide's (it will be recalled that *Service of All the Dead* was also set at a church named St. Frideswide's). The present church of St. Nicholas dates from the 12th century, with substantial additions from the 15th century.

The village played an important part in the Civil War, during the siege of Oxford. While the Royalist forces were besieged in the city, which had been used by King Charles I as his capital, the Parliamentary forces under Sir Thomas Fairfax had their headquarters in Marston, and used the church tower as a lookout post for viewing the enemy's artillery positions in what is now the University Parks.

[**The Victoria Arms where Morse recites _The Remorseful Day_**]

The Victoria Arms is a riverside public house sitting on the banks of the River Cherwell. Indeed the pub was the site of the old Marston rope ferry, which was the only way of getting from Marston and Headington to North Oxford and Summertown, until the construction of the Marston Ferry Link Road. The land and surrounding area is owned by the Oxford Preservation Trust and is carefully managed to keep a unique rural feeling despite being almost in Oxford city centre. Beyond are the hills of Wytham Woods over which the sun sets, and it was looking towards the sunset seated at a table on the terrace that Morse and Lewis discuss the case in _The Remorseful Day_. The scene is memorable since it ends with Morse reciting some lines from the A. E. Housmann poem of the episode title (a fact that is commemorated by a brass plaque inside the pub sponsored by The Inspector Morse Society and unveiled by Colin Dexter in 2003). A return visit to the same spot was made at the very end of the _Lewis_ episode

Expiation. Interestingly the geese that inhabit the field beyond the wall where Lewis and Hathaway are sitting were thought to detract from the scene so much that one of the film crew was given the task of crouching behind the wall holding the geese back so as to be out of shot. This is obviously a favourite drinking spot for Lewis since he returns here in three further episodes (*The Quality of Mercy, The Point of Vanishing* and *Falling Darkness*).

[The Hawkin's house in Old Marston]

The earliest history of the house now known as the Manor House is quite uncertain, but at least one book speaks of its 16th century character. This would have described the one house that is now split in two — the Manor House and Cromwell's House. What seems definite is that, in the times of King James I, a young man called Unkton Croke came down from his family home at Studley Priory and married a Marston heiress. He made her house 'grander', although a later writer called it 'a heavy stone building, erected without much attention to elegance or regularity'.

Croke was shrewd enough to support the Parliamentary cause during the Civil War, so that his house was the headquarters of General Fairfax during the siege of Oxford, and was visited by Oliver Cromwell, and may even have been used for the signing of the treaty following the siege.

Unkton Croke was a lawyer and seems to have prospered during the Protectorate to such an extent that, after the Restoration, he was obliged, and able, to put up a bond of £4,000 for the good behaviour of his Roundhead son.

The Croke family interest had ended by 1690, when the house was lived in by Thomas Rowney, another wealthy lawyer who, early in the 18ᵗʰ century, gave the land for the building of the Radcliffe Infirmary. However, both village and house must have fallen on hard times because it is said that by 1801 the house was used to home six pauper families, and subsequently prisoners of war from Napoleon's army are believed to have made carvings on the orchard wall which persist to this day.

In 1837, William Turner of Oxford painted a watercolour of the house, showing the 17ᵗʰ century facade with stone drip moulds, stone mullioned bay windows on the two floors and an attic floor with windows in the gable. In 1843 there was a fire which seriously damaged the front of, what is now known as, the Manor House, leaving Cromwell's House next door relatively untouched. The family owning the house at that time apparently then quarrelled and it was divided in two, with a wall built splitting the garden behind the houses, giving each half one pillar of the 17ᵗʰ century gate which had probably given access to the formal garden at that time. In the 20ᵗʰ century both houses have tended to have families enjoying long periods of ownership, and who have genuinely cared for the historic buildings with architectural features dating back many centuries.

In the *Lewis* episode *Falling Darkness* this was the setting for the house of Christine Hawkins (played by Joanna Roth).

THRUPP - THE BOAT INN

[The hamlet of Thrupp, just the place to find a headless corpse!]

Thrupp is a tiny hamlet midway between Kidlington and Shipton-on-Cherwell around ten miles north-west of Oxford. The first reference to Thrupp appears in the Domesday Book where it is recorded as Trop, the Old English for a farm or hamlet. Its size has not increased greatly since then, when the son of Wadard held it from Roger d'Ivry. Wadard was an officer of some importance in the Norman army and is pictured in the Bayeux Tapestry busying himself with supplies for the troops. The main attraction of Thrupp today is the row of picturesque terraced cottages along the bank of the Oxford Canal.

[The Boat Inn, conveniently located close to the scene of murder]

A mystery corpse is found here in *The Riddle of the Third Mile*. Morse, Lewis and Max (the pathologist), not surprisingly, retire to the Boat Inn for a whisky, after such an event. However, in the television adaptation of this story, *The Last Enemy*, the pathologist they meet at Thrupp is Grayling

Russell (played by Amanda Hillwood). Later in the adaptation Morse and Lewis return to seek professional advice as to which way and by how far the missing head may have travelled. Lewis seems a little distracted as he helps a young lady cast off, but both manage to pay a return visit to the Boat Inn.

WOODSTOCK - BLENHEIM PALACE THE MARLBOROUGH ARMS

[The magnificent entrance to Blenheim Palace]

Lying eight miles north of Oxford on the southern edge of the Cotswold Hills, Woodstock has been welcoming visitors since the time of King Henry II. Legend has it that King Alfred stayed here in the year 890 although the first firm evidence of a royal domicile is during the reign of Ethelred the Unready (976-1016) when he is known to have held at least one council (Witan) here. This suggests that there must have been either a lodge, or some sort of palace, large enough to accommodate the King and his entourage. The building does not stand today and it is not known where it stood. The arrival of the Normans brought about great changes to the countryside and its inhabitants. The sport of hunting became very important to the monarchy and large areas of forest were given over to hunting with the Saxon inhabitants being driven away. Those of the 'clearing in the woods' that was Woodstock were no exception and there is a strong belief that they were the founders of Old Woodstock which lies to the north of the River Glyme. The youngest son of William the Conqueror, King Henry I, is the first to be credited with enclosing what is now Blenheim Park and it is said that parts of the old wall can still be seen. After his death came nearly two decades of anarchy and civil war until the accession of King Henry II

(Plantagenet) in 1154. He was the first monarch to subdue the barons and unify the country under one authority. With his wife Eleanor D'Aquitaine, Henry Plantagenet held sway from England through to the Pyrenees in the South of France. He often stayed at Woodstock with his mistress 'The Fair Rosamund' (see under Godstow) and during the time he spent here granted parcels of land to build hostelries for the use of his men. A weekly market, on Tuesdays, was also established and a three day fair during the feast of St. Matthew.

The palace that stands today was built in 1715, being designed in a heavy Italo-Corinthian style by the architect Vanbrugh, and with the park being landscaped by Capability Brown. Most of the palace was paid for by the nation and was designated to John Churchill, the 1st Duke of Marlborough, in honour for his victories over the French and the Bavarians at Blenheim in 1704.

The greater part of the art treasures and curios were sold off in 1886, and the great library collected by Charles Spencer, Earl of Sunderland, the son-in-law of the 1st Duke of Marlborough, in 1881. The magnificent park contains Fair Rosamund's Well, near which stood her bower. On the summit of a hill stands a column commemorating the Duke. The palace was of course also the birthplace of one Winston Churchill.

With the building of the new palace came much new building in Woodstock itself and many of the old timber-framed structures were given new fronts of coursed stone and re-roofed using slate from nearby Stonesfield. Woodstock became renowned for the crafts, those of glove making and decorative steel work. Woodstock steel, said to be made from horseshoe nails, was cut to make jewellery and other decorative items.

Woodstock boasts several fine coaching inns including the 13th century Bear Hotel, the 14th century Marlborough Arms (currently an upmarket Bed & Breakfast establishment) and the 18th century Crown Inn. The Church of St. Mary Magdalene still retains its Norman doorway and some early English windows. The church is noted for its fine collection of kneelers of which there are over two hundred reflecting the life and interests of Woodstock.

In the television series Woodstock is naturally prominent in *The Last Bus to Woodstock*. In the book it is in the car park of the Black Prince public house where the body of Sylvia Kaye is found in suspicious circumstances, while in the television adaptation, the pub becomes the Fox and Castle and was actually shot in Surrey (see under Ockham).

[Left: The Marlborough Arms]

However, some of the scenes were also filmed at The Marlborough Arms, and this is certainly the place Colin Dexter had in mind since the layout closely fits the description in his book. It is a common mistake to think that the Black Prince of the book is the Black Prince by the river in Woodstock, but this public house only changed its name once the book had been published.

In *The Way Through the Woods*, Woodstock's Blenheim Palace is the employer of the blackmailing George Dale (played by Chris Fairbank) who later in the story is found dead on the estate. The placing of the body there is meant to throw Morse off the scent of the killers. Morse later interviews one of the suspects, Williams played by John Malcolm, in the park, with the Grand Bridge being clearly visible in the background. More recently scenes of Jessica Rattenbury's birthday party in the *Lewis* episode *The Point of Vanishing* were filmed here, including a murder in the maze that could have been mistaken for a scene in *Midsomer Murders*.

WYTHAM - WYTHAM WOODS
THE WHITE HART

[Part of the 960 acres of woods in which to conceal a body]

The woods take their name from the small stone-built village with many thatched cottages to the north-west of Oxford. The name is derived from the Old English words 'with', meaning bend, and 'ham', a village, estate or manor. It is an accurate description for Wytham lies near a sharp bend in the River Thames and has a manor which belonged to Abingdon Abbey.

It was held by the family of de Wytham from the 12th century until 1479 when it became the possession of the Harcourt family. After the dissolution of the monasteries it was bought by Lord Williams of Thame and in turn was passed to the Earls of Abingdon. The 7th Earl sold it to Raymond ffennell in 1920. The whole village is now owned by the University of Oxford who acquired the estate along with over 3,000 acres of land in 1943. This includes the 960 acres known as Wytham Woods. The main part of the woods is known as the 'Woods of Hazel' after Raymond ffennell's daughter, Hazel, who died at an early age. The woods are not open to the public (except for certain marked areas) as they are used for research by the University, who have a field station a mile to the north of the village.

Wytham Woods is a major backdrop for *The Way Through the Woods*. The search for 'The Swedish Maiden', Karin Anderson (played by Michelle Fairley), takes place here. A body is found, but it turns out to a male, that of photographer James Miteham. The blackmailing gardener, George Daley

85

(played by Chris Fairbank), also meets his fate here, at the woods' offices. Karin Anderson is eventually found here, very much alive, living under an alias as the wife of Dave Michaels (played by Neil Dudgeon who is now better known as Inspector John Barnaby in *Midsomer Murders*) in the gamekeeper's cottage. Although the woods were used in filming the cottage and climatic scenes in which Lewis is forced to dig his own grave were filmed in Surrey. Interestingly enough this episode mirrored real life events for in 1960 an Oxford woman was found dead in the woods after having been missing for two weeks. It was Karen Maas, the Danish wife of a classics professor at the University. However, this is where the similarity ends for there was no suspicion of foul play in this case.

[Courtyard of The White Hart in Wytham]

Also in *The Way Through the Woods* the White Hart public house in the village of Wytham is used as a location for the usual drink and discussion between Morse and Lewis. Morse is rather bad-tempered on this occasion and simply asks Lewis to buy him (naturally Morse would not be paying!) "whatever the locals drink". The pub was also used much earlier in the series in filming *The Secret of Bay 5B*.

INSPECTOR MORSE IN SOMERSET
BATH - ROYAL CRESCENT HOTEL

[The Royal Crescent, architecture to rival even that of Oxford]

Bath has a population of around eighty thousand persons and was made a county borough in 1889 that gave it administrative independence from its county, Somerset. The city became part of Avon when that county was created in 1974 but since 1996, when Avon was abolished, Bath has again been part of Somerset.

The city was founded, among surrounding hills, in the valley of the River Avon around naturally occurring hot springs where the Romans built baths and a temple, giving it the name *Aquae Sulis*. Bath became popular as a spa resort during the Georgian era, which led to a major expansion that left a heritage of exemplary Georgian architecture crafted from Bath stone. Indeed the city became a World Heritage Site in 1987.

The Royal Crescent is a notable residential road of thirty houses, laid out in a crescent. It was designed by the architect John Wood the Younger, and built between 1767 and 1774. It is amongst the greatest examples of Georgian architecture to be found in the United Kingdom and is a Grade I listed building. Together with his father John Wood, the Elder, John Wood the Younger was interested in the occult and masonic symbolism. It has been suggested that their creation of the Royal Crescent and the nearby Circus (originally King's Circus), that from the air can be observed to be a giant circle and crescent, is actually symbolic of the *soleil-lune*, the sun and moon. Further the Circus, along with Gay Street and Queens Square, forms a key shape, which is of course a masonic symbol.

87

The houses in Royal Crescent are a mixture of tenures ranging from privately owned to a substantial minority being run by a housing association. Today many residences have been converted into flats. Two notable exceptions are No. 1 Royal Crescent which is a museum maintained by the Bath Preservation Trust, and No. 15 (at the very centre) which is the entrance to the luxury Royal Crescent Hotel (which also occupies No. 16). The entrance leads to the front reception rooms but behind this is the beautiful and completely secluded hidden 'secret' garden leading to what would have been the coach houses, which are now occupied by individual bedrooms and suites (each of which is named after an illustrious person associated with the city, and include Sir Thomas Gainsborough and Jane Austen), the exclusive spa and the Dower House restaurant and bar.

The Wrong Box (1966) and *The Remains of the Day* (1993) as well as the BBC adaptation of *Persuasion* all made good use of the location for filming. It is certainly the hotel of choice for Morse for it is where at the end of *Death is Now My Neighbour* that he takes Adele Cecil (played by Judy Loe) telling the porter who is taking their bags from the Jaguar that he will have no further need of his car that evening. The Royal Crescent is one of those locations in which the Jaguar seems to be so much at home. The hotel is also where the Storrs stay for a weekend conference at Bath. Finally it is in the 'secret' garden that Colin Dexter makes his usual Hitchcock-like appearance in this episode.

INSPECTOR MORSE IN SURREY

HORSELL - THE CRICKETERS

[A good place to study Ancient Greek?]

Horsell is a village on the outskirts of Woking, probably best known because of its association with the story *The War of the Worlds*, written by H. G. Wells for it was close to here that the attack from Mars made its first strike. It is also the home of Horsell Cricket Club, whose members have included Alec and Eric Bedser, the twins who played cricket for England. It is no surprise then to find a public house called the Cricketers that in the *Lewis* episode *Whom the Gods Would Destroy* is where Lewis and Hathaway go to try and understand the notes, made in Greek, by the departed Dean Greely (played by Crispin Redman).

OCKHAM - THE BLACK SWAN

Ockham is close to East Horsley and appears in the Domesday book as Bocheham. It was the birthplace of William of Ockham, famous philosopher and the proponent of Occam's Razor.

Ockham Common, to the north-east of the village, is the site of the disused Wisley Airfield. Although the airfield is no longer, the aviation connection remains, being the location of 'OCK', a navigational beacon that anchors the south-west arrival stack for London Heathrow airport. Close to the common is found the Black Swan public house. In the episode entitled *The Last Bus to Woodstock* this pub became the site for the Fox and Castle and is where the body of Sylvia Kane (played by Jenny Jay) is found dead in the car park.

[One Morse pub where you should always check your rear view mirror before reversing in the car park]

Pyrford & Ripley – Newark Priory
The Seven Stars

Close to the village of Pyrford, and beside the River Wey, is Newark Priory. It was established in the late 12th century by Rauld de Calva and his wife Beatrice de Saudes for Augustian canons, and was dedicated to the Virgin Mary and Thomas Beckett and was a *novo loco* (a new place for monks from nearby). The Priory's name changed over the years to Newstead and then finally to Newark. During King Henry VIII's Dissolution of the Monasteries Newark Priory was indeed dissolved. The prior was pensioned off with valuables being sent to the Tower of London and the land given over to the Master of the King's Horse. It has been said that a cannon was employed from the top of Church Hill to bombard, what were, the then extensive buildings. The last known prior of Newark Priory was Richard Lipscombe, appointed just before the surrender of the house in 1538. The buildings fell into ruin, and were said to have been further destroyed by locals using the stones for road mending; until Lord Onslow, the owner in the 1730s, decided to preserve what remained.

[A quiet ruin and just the place to find a dead body]

Today Newark Priory is still a ruin and is listed as a Grade I Ancient Monument, and also upon the English Heritage register of buildings at risk. It appears twice as a filming location for *Inspector Morse*. The first is in *The Wolvercote Tongue* since it is here that a picnicking couple find the naked body of Theodore Kemp (played by Simon Callow) that has been beached after having tumbled over a weir (supposedly on the River Cherwell), while in *Twilight of the Gods* the river changes to the Isis and is again the scene for a body being found. This time it is that of journalist Neville Grimshaw (uncredited) who is discovered in a punt.

A return to the area was made in the *Lewis* episode *The Great and the Good* when the Seven Stars public house at Ripley became a stand in for the Bookbinders Arms that it will be recalled was originally featured in *The Dead of Jericho*.

VIRGINIA WATER - HOLLOWAY SANATORIUM

[Entrance to the Great Hall]

The site of the old Holloway Sanatorium is the present Virginia Park gated residential development in Virginia Water, on the west side of Stroude Road and to the north of the railway station. It was one of two important symbols of the vision of the Victorian multi-millionaire entrepreneur and philanthropist, Thomas Holloway (1800-1883): the other being the nearby Royal Holloway College in Egham (now part of the University of London). Like the college, the sanatorium was an extraordinary and extensive building, founded and personally funded by Holloway as a 'gift to the Nation', and it was the fruit of the partnership between Holloway and his principal architect William Henry Crossland. The architecture was inspired by the Gothic styles of the Cloth Hall of Ypres in Belgium with its conspicuous tower, and the *Sainte-Chapelle* in Paris. Work started on the building of the sanatorium in 1873. The institution, 'a hospital for the insane of the middle class', was opened by the Prince and Princess of Wales (later King Edward VII and Queen Alexandra) in 1885. There were seventy-three certified patients admitted in the first year, and the number increased steadily so that in 1892 it already exceeded its capacity for six hundred patients. A board of trustees managed the Sanatorium until it passed to the National Health Service in 1948. It closed in 1981 and soon became derelict, vandalised and pillaged for the next dozen years when work began on its restoration. It reopened in 2000 and although not open to the public there are open days, organised by English Heritage, almost every month when visitors are allowed into the Great Hall.

Morse was no stranger to the Holloway Sanatorium since in *The Dead of Jericho* he attends choir rehearsals here (albeit arriving late at the very end of practice), while in *The Silent World of Nicholas Quinn* the location doubles as the inquest court where Christopher Roope (played by Anthony Smee) is (incorrectly) arrested.

INSPECTOR MORSE IN THE WEST MIDLANDS

DUDLEY - BLACK COUNTRY LIVING MUSEUM

[Just part of the Black Country Living Museum showing where the *Barbara Bray* began her fateful journey]

The Black Country Living Museum is an open-air museum of rebuilt historic buildings occupying some 26 acres. It was first opened in 1976, on land partly reclaimed from a former railway goods yard, disused limekilns and former coal pits; and since then many more exhibits have been added to it. Most of the buildings are original but have been relocated from elsewhere.

Electric trams and trolleybuses transport visitors from the entrance in a recreated factory to the village area with thirty buildings situated by the canal basin. Coalmine displays include underground workings, colliery surface buildings and a replica of the 1712 Newcomen steam engine. In all, forty-two separate displays have either been re-erected or built to old plans to create a living open-air museum.

Houses, shops and public buildings have been rebuilt to create a single early 20th century street, peopled by staff in period costume. Some of these buildings are still used in their original function, such as the public house, the sweet shop and the church. Others are faithful replicas of their last use, with goods in the windows. Still others are only shells of the originals, such as the bathhouse. By immersing the visitor in the everyday objects of life, it becomes clearer how things connected.

Visitors to the museum may also take a narrow boat trip on the adjacent canal, through the Dudley Tunnel, or enjoy a traditional lesson in the schoolroom, or even go into a mine. The museum is certainly worth a whole days visit.

It was quite evidently the Victorian surroundings coupled with the waterside location that made the museum an obvious choice for filming some of the boat scenes (supposedly Coventry) in *The Wench is Dead.*

-- --- ·-· ··· ·

INSPECTOR MORSE IN WILTSHIRE
HONEYSTREET - THE BARGE INN

[The Barge Inn, little altered since it was rebuilt in 1859]

The Barge Inn is at the epicentre of a plethora of ancient sites and tracks. It is close to the beginning of the Ridgeway, one of the oldest highways in the country dating back to the stone age, a few miles from the Avebury stone circle, the bronze age cathedral to Stonehenge's parish church and Silbury, the unexplained, manmade hill on the side of the A4 and just down the road from the West Kennet Long Barrow.

Nearby the Norman churches of St. Mary the Virgin in Alton Barnes and All Saints in Alton Priors are well worth a visit as is the war memorial that is found a few hundred yards down the towpath from the public house.

The Barge Inn itself has a long and colourful history, built in 1810 to coincide with the opening of the Kennet and Avon Canal, it prospered alongside a waterway then busy with both commercial and passenger traffic. Known in its heyday as the George, the establishment contained a slaughter house, coach house and stabling for four horses, as well as a brew house, hop store, bake house, smoke house and cart shed. The north section

97

of the ground floor included a grocery and general stores, as between 1871 and 1957 a number of licensees also acted as local grocers.

Sadly, fire broke out on the 14th December 1858 largely destroying the original building and preceding what the *Devizes & Wiltshire Gazette* referred to as a 'disgraceful scene. Soon after the fire was extinguished ... the cellars were entered ... and there was nothing but drunkenness and confusion'.

However, due to its importance, the Barge Inn was rebuilt in just six months, an event commemorated by a plaque at the north gable end. The inn, which now had no fewer than twenty-four rooms within the main building and fifteen fireplaces including those in the bake house and barns, flourished along with other services at Honeystreet such as the sawmills, builders wharf and coal stores.

The canal became more neglected with the arrival of the railways, but this did not prevent the place from being sold by auction on Wednesday 7th April 1897 ('at three o'clock punctually'), to T. & J. Usher of Bristol, for the then considerable sum of £2,100. Today, a hundred years later, the wheel of history has turned full circle: the present owners, re-acquiring the establishment in 1992, are the well-known Ushers of Trowbridge.

This transaction was marginally preceded by the mysterious appearance of crop circles in the vicinity, causing many students of these phenomena to swell the ranks of customers who include cyclists, walkers, canoeists, narrow boat enthusiasts and occasionally musicians.

In June 1998 the Barge Inn was host to Carlton Television's production of *The Wench is Dead*. It was selected as the perfect location for the flashback scenes to 1853 that required a building that hadn't been altered since its erection in 1810. Initially the production team dressed the pub, covered the tarmac, overhead cables and aerials along with props including carts, a flock of chickens, cart horses, rabbits and other props of the period. In addition to this it is also the public house to which Morse and Lewis retire in the same episode to discuss the case once the former has been discharged from hospital. If in the vicinity it is certainly to be recommended for a visit whether for the atmosphere of the eccentrics who frequent the bar, the tranquil setting, the good food, the nearby walks along the canal, or the view of White Horse of Alton Barnes carved out on the hill.

INSPECTOR MORSE FURTHER AFIELD

Although most of the location filming for *Inspector Morse* and *Lewis* takes place in the Home Counties with much of that being based in and around Oxford itself there were times when the production team went much further afield from Morse's fictional home.

AUSTRALIA

Apart from some of the opening shots at Kensal Green in London (see under Brent, London) the entire *Promised Land* episode was shot in Australia. At the end of the episode there are some pretty standard shots of the Sydney Opera House as Morse walks up the steps to attend Richard Strauss's *Der Rosenkavalier*. The various other scenes though were filmed several hours drive away at Canowindra and Cowra in New South Wales. Canowindra was the fictional town of Hereford with Gaskill Street standing in for the main shopping street in Hereford. Most memorable though are the climatic scenes at the disused railway station. This wasn't one of the best episodes for plot (although there was some superlative acting from John Thaw) as it is generally thought that it was a bit of a 'jolly boys' outing'. Indeed even Lewis questions the logic of him having to go to Australia but is told by Morse that "I can't carry my own bags, can I? I'm a chief inspector".

GERMANY

In the *Lewis* episode *Music to Die For* it is Hathaway who gets to do the travelling, albeit for a day trip it seems, to Berlin. There are some standard shots of the Brandenburger Tor and in front of the main railway station around Alexanderplatz.

ITALY

In the episode entitled *The Death of the Self* filming locations around Verona and Vicenza were used extensively and to great effect. It does seem that whenever Morse has to travel abroad for work that there is always an opera facility close at hand. This story goes one better and includes an opera singer as a main character. Morse arrives at Vicenza railway station where he comments to Lewis that even the station announcer sounds like music to his ears. He then proceeds to check into his hotel (which is actually the luxury Due Torri Hotel Baglioni in Verona) but when he opens his bedroom window he is greeted with a view of Vicenza! Good use was made of the Basillica Palladiana (which doubled as the police station) and surrounding central area of Vicenza. Two private properies, Villa Franceschini Canera di Salasco and Villa Pisani, were used as the homes of

Nicole Burgess (played by Frances Barber) and Russell Clarke (Michael Kitchen) respectively.

[**Villa Franceschini Canera di Salasco where you can 'burn the past'**]

Finally the Arena di Verona, a Roman amphitheatre with a seating capacity of twenty-two thousand, was used for both the rehearsal and performance of *Turandot* towards the end of this episode. Again there are those who would say that this was another 'jolly boys' outing' and even if this is so it is a very beautifully shot outing with some memorable dialogue and interplay between the main proponents.

WALES

At the conclusion of *The Wench is Dead* Morse tests out his theory that Charles Franks (played by Kieran Aherne), otherwise known as illusionist the Great Donovan, faked his own death as an insurance fraud, by tracking down his place of burial in Ireland and having his coffin opened only to find it full of rocks, thus confirming his theory. The actual location of the church and cemetery beside the sea is St. Hywyns Church, Aberdaron in Wales.

INSPECTOR MORSE ON LOCATION MAPS

The following maps are merely intended to show the relative positions of the various locations covered in the text and are not meant to be to scale. The associated tables give both the type of place according to the defined symbols in the table below, along with the page number in brackets for that location. In so doing it is hoped that the maps will help the reader when planning their own visits to these places of interest.

Key to Symbols

 **Building (General)**	 **Building (Large/Important)**	 **Church (Religious Establishment)**
 **Museum (Tourist Attraction)**	 **Park/Garden/Wood**	 **Place of Learning (School/Library)**
 **Public House/ Hotel/Brewery**	 **Railway Related**	

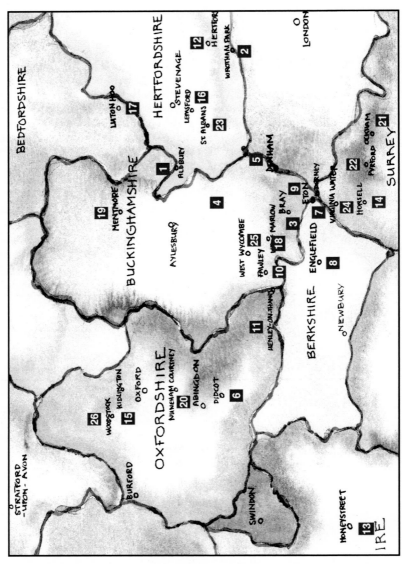

Map 1 – Inspector Morse on Location in Central England

Key to Map 1

1	Aldbury (32)		14	Horsell (89)	
2	Barnet (34)		15	Kidlington (74)	
3	Bray (11)		16	Lemsford (38)	
4	Chenies (19)		17	Luton (9)	
5	Denham (20)		18	Marlow (24)	
6	Didcot (68)		19	Mentmore (26)	
7	Dorney (22)		20	Nuneham Courtney (76)	
8	Englefield (15)		21	Ockham (89)	
9	Eton (17)		22	Pyrford & Ripley (90)	
10	Fawley (23)		23	St. Albans (40)	
11	Henley-on-Thames (72)		24	Virginia Water (92)	
12	Hertford (36)		25	West Wycombe (27)	
13	Honeystreet (97)		26	Woodstock (82)	

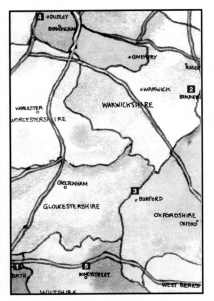

Key to Map 2

1	Bath (87)	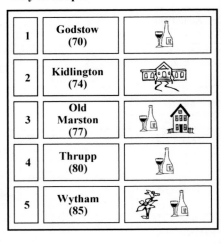
2	Braunston (65)	
3	Burford (67)	
4	Dudley (95)	
5	Honeystreet (97)	

Map 2 – Inspector Morse on Location in Western England

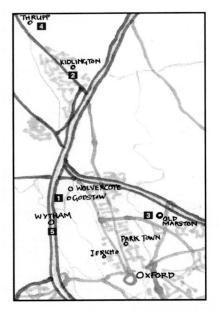

Key to Map 3

1	Godstow (70)	
2	Kidlington (74)	
3	Old Marston (77)	
4	Thrupp (80)	
5	Wytham (85)	

Map 3 – Inspector Morse on Location in North Oxford

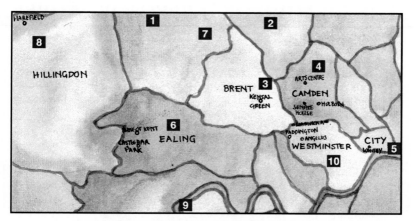

Map 4 – Inspector Morse on Location in London

Key to Map 4

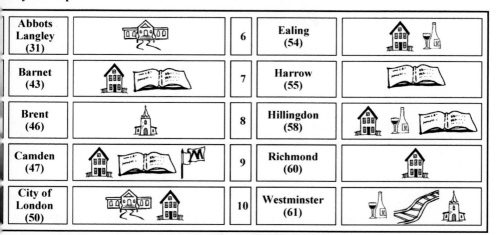

Abbots Langley (31)		6	**Ealing (54)**		
Barnet (43)		7	**Harrow (55)**		
Brent (46)		8	**Hillingdon (58)**		
Camden (47)		9	**Richmond (60)**		
City of London (50)		10	**Westminster (61)**		

105

ENJOYED THIS PUBLICATION?
THEN YOU SHOULD BUY OUR COMPANION VOLUME

THE OXFORD OF INSPECTOR MORSE

All the Central Oxford Locations

Includes Location Map and Walking Guide

Includes *Inspector Morse* and *Lewis*

Original Bestselling Guide Fully Illustrated

From the Ashmolean Museum to the White Horse, *The Oxford of Inspector Morse* is the original and bestselling guide to the various Oxford locations most associated with the books and television productions of Inspector Morse (and *Lewis*).

It not only gives the *Inspector Morse* and *Lewis* connections but concentrates on the historical aspects of more than thirty places used in filming the adventures. This 76 page booklet is now in its tenth edition, updated, fully illustrated, with location map and Oxford walk. This publication features at number six in the **Blackwell's Bestseller List.**

Published in association with
The Inspector Morse Society

A must for any Inspector Morse, Lewis or Oxford enthusiast

ISBN 978-1901091-03-8 – R.R.P. £5.00 (including P&P)

Available from all good bookshops or direct from the Society:
The Inspector Morse Society, Endeavour House, 170 Woodland Road,
Sawston, Cambridgeshire CB22 3DX
www.inspector-morse.com

PLACES INDEX

Miscellaneous

EPISODE INDEX

109

REFERENCES & CREDITS

Allen, Paul & Allen, Jan, *Endeavouring to Crack the Morse Code*, 372 pages, Exposure Publishing, (2007), ISBN: 978-1846855115. Interesting subject matter but appallingly written and produced with literally hundreds of errors.

Bird, Christopher, *The World of Inspector Morse*, 160 pages, Boxtree Limited, (1998), ISBN: 978-0752221175. A complete A-Z reference for the Morse enthusiast with foreword by Colin Dexter. Several mistakes but still remains one of the best guides to *Inspector Morse* available.

Bishop, David, *The Complete Inspector Morse*, 296 pages, Titan Books, (2011), ISBN: 978-0857682482. Attempts to be the last word on *Inspector Morse* and *Lewis* containing a critique of all the novels, television adaptations, and other writers' stories featuring the popular characters. A default guide for any enthusiast.

Earwaker, Julian & Becker, Kathleen, *Scene of the Crime*, 256 pages, Aurum Press Limited, (2002), ISBN: 978-1854108210. A superb work surveying the landscapes of British detective fiction. Although broad in content this guide is not comprehensive within a particular author or location.

Godwin, John, & Richards, Antony J. with introduction by Colin Dexter, *The Murder of Christina Collins*, 62 pages, Irregular Special Press, (2011), ISBN: 978-1901091441. Definitive guide to the real life murder of Christina Collins on the Trent and Mersey Canal at Rugeley, Staffordshire in 1839. It was upon this event that Colin Dexter based his book *The Wench Is Dead*.

Goodwin, Cliff, *Inspector Morse Country*, 224 pages, Headline Book Publishing, (2002), ISBN: 978-0755310647. A beautifully produced tribute to the world of Oxford's famous detective. Well illustrated with many useful addresses and other information. An essential part of any *Inspector Morse* collection.

Hibbert, Christopher (Editor) & Hibbert, Edward (Associate Editor), 562 pages, *The Encyclopaedia of Oxford*, Macmillan, (1988), ISBN: 978-0333399170. Essential reading for anybody interested in the history of Oxford.

Honey, Derek, *An Encyclopaedia of Oxford Pubs, Inns and Taverns*, 128 pages, Oakwood Press, (1998), ISBN: 978-0853615354. An informative guide, with foreword by Colin Dexter, to over 700 establishments along with mention of those most frequented by Inspector Morse.

Leonard, Bill, *The Oxford of Inspector Morse and Lewis*, 192 pages, The History Press, (2008), ISBN: 978-0752446219. Despite being full of information, often minutiae, relating to *Inspector Morse* and Oxford it is poorly produced, overpriced and relies heavily on information already published elsewhere. The text is set out non-logically and the photographs amateurish. Such a pity as this should have been a definitive guide to *Inspector Morse* locations.

Richards, Antony & Attwell, Philip, *The Oxford of Inspector Morse*, 76 pages, Irregular Special Press, (2007), ISBN: 978-1901091038. Now in its tenth edition, and designed to complement this publication, this best selling booklet covers over thirty *Inspector Morse* and *Lewis* central Oxford locations. The guide is fully illustrated and comes with a walking guide and map.

Sanderson, Mark, *The Making of Inspector Morse*, 144 pages, Pan Books, (1995), ISBN 978-0330344188. A classic guide to the filming of the series that should be on every *Inspector Morse* enthusiast's shelf.

Weinreb, Ben (Editor) & Hibbert, Christopher (Editor), *The London Encyclopaedia*, 1120 pages, MacMillan Reference, (2010), ISBN: 978-1405049252. Quite simply the definitive and most comprehensive book on London ever published.

Morse in Oxford, 32 pages, Pitkin Publishing, (2009), ISBN 978-1841652276. A colourful but very lightweight publication that only covers the main tourist areas of Oxford in a superficial manner. Comes with a CD of in the main non-Morse related classical music.

The cover illustration and maps are by Nikki Sims. The author would like to acknowledge Colin Dexter, Philip Attwell and Heather Chisholme for all the help and inspiration they have given towards this publication.

WHY NOT JOIN THE INSPECTOR MORSE SOCIETY?
www.inspector-mores.com